RICH

in

Happiness

7 Steps to Living Happily
For the Rest of Your Life

Alex J. Kim

Rich in Happiness: 7 Steps to Living Happily for the Rest of Your Life.

Bopyo Press Edition
Visit our Web site at www.bopyo.com

ISBN-13: 978-0692220351

Library of Congress Cataloging in Publication Data.

1.Happiness. 2. Health. 3. Self-improvement (Psychology).

Published in association with Bopyo LLC.
Design and illustrations by Alex J. Kim.

Acknowledgements

To my wife Pamela for her love, inspiration, and creativity which made this book possible.

To our children Enaka and Adora, and to future generations.

To my parents for their demonstration of love and a standard of excellence.

To all who fight to find happiness and are willing to pay its price.

Contents

WORLD'S #1 PROBLEM

Introduction

My childhood was filled with fun and laughter. Life was simple, yet loaded with thrills such as playing sports, making plastic models, and reading comics. I especially liked exploring nature around me. Summer vacations were most memorable because that was the time to run around the fields, sneak into neighbor's apple orchards, catch frogs, and collect insects.

Story times with my grandma were a sheer delight as well. Most of them were fables and ridiculous stories she made up on a whim, but we didn't care; they were all fun. My grandma—she was a beautiful woman. There were many great traits about her, but distinctly she was one of those rare people who was constantly cheerful. She was always thrilled to see people, and they felt her genuineness and warmth. No matter who you were, she made you feel special. If I was to point out a happy individual whom I met over my lifetime, it would be grandma.

The glow of childhood gradually dimmed however, as I grew and took on responsibilities and faced the walls of life's disappointments. I rarely got depressed up to my teens, but then circumstances changed. While studying Economics at the University of Washington in Seattle, I began to seriously question whether happiness was attainable in this life.

I was depressed, wondering about the purpose of life, my career choices, and longing for meaningful relationships. At times thoughts danced in my mind suggesting it was better to die than live like this.

During those years I experienced dark times, but I also experienced peaks of happiness difficult to describe in words. Still I struggled to keep peak experiences on a consistent basis. I didn't know deep seated joy that is continuous and tangible was possible, but it was worth the try—I decided to risk everything for it. I was determined to find ways to be joyful no matter what the circumstances might be.

So I began to read all the books and listen to audios I could get my hands on about living happily. I went around asking so many questions, some people even avoided being around me. What I heard, observed, learned—I collected on notepads, napkins, or even on my hands. Many times insights came just as I laid down to sleep—at such times I forced myself to get up and capture them. At times understanding flowed at such a speed I couldn't write fast enough. I made it my life's goal to reach that state. Thomas Edison had his ten thousand experiments before he came across the bulb that lit up. I was committed to light up my own heart so I could light up other hearts in the world.

I have learned the lack of happiness is a common plague in the world. In fact, it has been and is the world's number one problem. At the beginning I didn't know there were principles of happiness. I thought people had to accept feeling meager and just bear it. Many people may believe that way. Since then I have learned it is possible to attain happiness that rises above life's circumstances. What is required is change of habits—starting with one's mind and beliefs. Like growing a lovely flower, attaining happiness takes attention and action.

In order to get the most out of this book:

1. Underline or mark areas that speak to you; distinguish them according to their importance.
2. Review this book regularly so its principles are always fresh in your mind.
3. Apply the principles in this book at every opportunity. If you don't, you will forget them and lose your efforts. Understanding only comes if you apply your knowledge, and knowledge only sticks if it gets used.

This book has been twenty years in the making. It has taken that long to research, learn, and apply these timeless principles of happiness in my own life. I also see them work in many others where happiness is something they experience on a daily basis. In my professional career, I worked as a Data Analyst for one of the Fortune 100 companies. Research and analysis comes naturally for me, and became helpful in writing this book.

I enjoyed comics and illustrating growing up, so I shook the dust off my pen and injected cartoons in these pages to further enhance comprehension and fun. I hope you enjoy viewing them as much as I have delighted in drawing them. You will notice I slapped my sense of humor on them as well.

During the course of writing this book, my daughter Adora was born. As I held her, I was reminded it was not just her body but her future which lay in my hands. What kind of life can I give her? Inheritances are passed on to children by parents, but what can be more valuable than being rich in happiness? Isn't happiness the supreme gift and what every parent desires for their children? I believe it is not the responsibility of parents to pave the road for their children, but to provide a road map. In the following chapters we will explore seven rich principles for a lifetime of happiness.

My child, let me help you feel the sunshine of happiness.
Feel it in spite of life's storms and life's calm.
See its glow, experience its warmth.
Here, stand on my shoulders so you can reach high.
Let me behold your smile's worth.
For your joy is my delight and the apple of my eye.

CHAPTER 1

You Can Learn to be Happy

Everything we do is to fill up our measures of happiness: go to work, develop friendships, buy things, and reach for dreams. In fact, every thought and decision we make is ultimately for the outcome of personal happiness. People are scrambling and laboring so hard to find it. When I consider our current society, I see people riding on one another's necks and pressing one another to death to get foremost in this race called life. Yet, people are not satisfied.

Observe and you will see this dissatisfaction all around. People who own Mercedes are no happier than owners of GMs. Those who live in bigger houses are no happier than those who live in small ones. Powerful and influential people are no more satisfied than average citizens. Cover girls are no happier than plain women; in fact, they may be less happy.

A counselor had a patient who was as beautiful as any woman he had ever seen, in magazines or in the movies. She was intelligent and charismatic. But she spent her life being tormented by the possibility she may come across another woman who was more beautiful than she. He also dealt with a large number of extremely wealthy people and observed that they were perhaps some of the most miserable clients he had ever encountered.

In the autobiography of the famous basketball player Wilt Chamberlain, he wrote he enjoyed sexual relationships with what he guessed to be over a thousand women.[1] One may well guess some of these women probably were quite good at sensual arts. Why wouldn't ten suffice, or even twenty?

Kings and presidents lust for more power and cause wars. The wealthiest embezzle to get more. Even with all they have, they struggle to be happy. In our day some of the most influential people have died attempting to fill their void, but the wrong way—people like Elvis Presley, Whitney Houston, and Heath Ledger. We have seen billionaires and even top leaders of nations taking their own lives.

If left untreated, the void of happiness can result not only in the death of oneself but of others as well. I will boldly state this, *it is usually those who are hurting who hurt others. Truly happy people have no reason but to love.*

People have different personalities and some are prone to be more optimistic and happier than others. However I would like to emphasize, happiness is primarily what we learn. It is a matter of discarding bad habits and replacing them with good and healthy ones.

Some people are also born into better circumstances or with better physical conditions than others, but if you choose to apply the principles of happiness that are presented in this book and seek to live differently from the majority of mankind, you can be happier than those who may have had those things handed to them.

The benefits of happiness are all encompassing. Research reveals that happiness promotes enhanced brain functioning and better memory.[2] On the other hand, depression, fear, and stress paralyze both the mind and the body. Healthy emotion impacts every area of one's life: mental, physical, relational, financial, etc. When happy, you think and act better. That is why the happier you are the more successful you will be. The reward of our pursuit of happiness is worth its weight in gold—certainly it is a goal worthy of our highest endeavor. I am confident if you apply the principles shared in this book, you will be happier, more excited, and more successful than you have ever been before.

CHAPTER 2

How Happy Are You?

If you would be happy for three hours, get drunk.
If you would be happy for three days, roast a pig.
If you would be happy for three months, get married.
If you would be happy for a lifetime, plant a garden.

~ Chinese proverb ~

Many people don't believe happiness is possible, or for those who do believe the way toward it appears puzzling and complex.

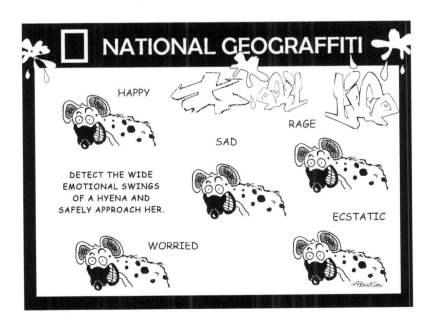

Everyone goes through different mood changes, from valley to mountain peak experiences. Wouldn't it be wonderful if you lived at the peak of happiness everyday? Although that may be difficult to achieve, I believe living most of your life near happiness peak is possible. And that is the destination we want to reach by the end of this book.

Before you go anywhere you have to know where you are first. So let's first measure your present level of happiness. Look at the Happiness Scale below. It has ratings from zero to ten. A score of zero means you are extremely unhappy most of the time. A rating of ten means you are extremely happy, that you live in the state of ecstasy where you just don't know what to do with yourself!

Rate yourself on the scale. You can do this by drawing a vertical line and dating above the number between 0 and 10 on the scale.

Happiness Scale

0 1	2 3	4 5 6	7 8	9 10
Completely depressed	More depressed than happy	Happy half the time	Happy most of the time	Extremely happy

If you find yourself on the lower part of the scale, don't be discouraged. You are among the majority of people. Continue to plot along the scale as you apply the principles mentioned in this book and make gradual progress. Only make sure that you live deliberately to be happy.

CHAPTER 3

Causes of Unhappiness

People ask where depression comes from. They get as varied and often silly answers as those given by children when asked, "Where do babies come from?" Kids think babies come from fat ladies, mom's butt, or peanuts. Here are some of the funniest:

"My two and a half year old thinks this baby is coming out of my belly button. He comes up and squeezes everyday to see if the baby will come out of there but to no avail. "

"When I was a little girl I was told that you get pregnant from eating a watermelon seed. Talk about terrifying!"

"One day my little brother proudly announced that he knew where babies came from. So my dad asked him where that was and he explained...when a mommy and daddy decided to have a baby they choose if they want a boy or a girl and then the doctor takes one of daddy's balls and puts it in mommy. One ball is a boy and one is a girl...my dad asked how that might happen because he has two daughters and three sons. My brother responded, 'Well they grow back silly!'"

One of my friends had his sister adopted internationally when he was around 6 years old. He told me that he was very excited and vividly remembers seeing her sister handed over to his parents. So for a long time he thought babies came from airports!

Now, where does depression come from? Before we can look at principles that invigorate happiness we need to first briefly identify where depression comes from. There are various causes of unhappiness; I will list some of the major ones here:

- Selfishness
- Lust

- Anger
- Unbalanced Lifestyle
- Worry
- Guilt
- Legalism or Lawlessness
- Engaging Life Too Seriously
- Burnout

Selfishness

How many people do you know who are selfish and happy? Probably none. There is a lot of talk about dealing with oneself—from magazines, to books, to songs. And it seems those who are trying to guide in this area are as confused as those who are looking for answers. Many have suffered from false guidance. So first of all let us make some clarifications:

Selfishness is not proper self-respect and love.
Selfishness is the exact opposite of love.

Let's distinguish selfishness and self-care. Selfishness is bad but self-care and self-respect is good. There is not an adequate word in the English language to describe proper care of self—one that is selfless and at the same time aptly taking care of oneself in a healthy way. In an airplane it is a loving act to put the air mask on yourself first before putting it on your child so that you can save your child—that is the smart thing to do. Outward appearance means nothing, motivation is everything. The nature of the two is distinctly different and you will experience these separate traits amidst your actions when you are doing one or the other:

Selfishness is possessive, hypersensitive, impulsive, fearful, and is always accompanied by depression.

Self-respect is simple, peaceful, gentle, outgoing, freeing, dignifying, and joyful.

Another common term for selfishness is narcissism, named after the young man in Greek mythology, Narcissus. In the story Narcissus was very handsome, and because of it he was exceptionally proud and disdained others. One day Narcissus went to a pool where he saw his own reflection in the water and fell in love with it, not realizing it was merely an image. Unable to leave the beauty of his reflection, Narcissus died.

Selfishness can be compared to cancer. A cancer cell is one that seeks to live and spread while killing other cells. Selfishness does a great deal of harm to one's soul and body.

FOR THE FIRST TIME IN HISTORY
A MICROSCOPE THAT CAN AMPLIFY
UP TO 100,000X REVEALED CANCER CELLS IN ACTION.

The golden rule states, "In everything treat others the same way you want them to treat you." Proper self-awareness and treatment is doing unto ourselves what we would do unto others: in love, kindness, respect, honor, and praise. We cannot love others unless we properly love, respect, and take care of ourselves.

TIP

Childhood is the most impressionable stage in our growth. What we learn and receive as children (especially up through grade school level) can set behavioral patterns or habits that can last a lifetime. It is this stage where receiving love is most vital. *Those who receive love see themselves as being lovely; they also learn how to give love. In turn, they are able to love others.*

If you mistreat others it is partly because you mistreat yourself as well. As you develop a healthy self-respect you'll be able to trust in yourself, your own judgment, and affectively love others.

Lust

Lust blinds.

Patrick was a troubled young man when he went to see a counselor. In his adolescence, he had sexual fantasies about girls in bathing suits. He then moved to photography magazines which contained nude models. But these didn't arouse him for long, so he progressed to low-key pornography. Being underage he had to pay a high price to get them from friends who had access to them. When soft-core failed to give him a thrill, he graduated to hard-core porn.

In his early twenties he married. But his desire for pornography didn't fade away, in fact it increased. The hardcore porn lost its fizzle, so he began visiting strip shows. When his craving for perverse thrills got increasingly worse and dark, he sought therapy.[1]

Lust however, is not limited to the sexual arena; it can involve money, power, or even romantic relationships. Lust, addiction, jealousy, and greed all have common grounds—your mind constantly dwells on the object of your affection, and your emotions become consumed by it. It doesn't matter if it involves someone or something. In the state of lust you are constantly wanting but not being able to have, so inside you there is a constant inner turmoil. You can't have lust in your life and experience peace and inner satisfaction.

Question:
But can't I enjoy the good feeling that comes with consuming lust and then turn it off to experience peace and happiness whenever I want to? Or at least have peace and joy the majority of the time?

Answer:
No, *because they both* are a *lifestyle*.
You can't switch from one to the other.
You cannot have peace without losing lust and vice versa.
Lust and peace in your life are contrary to one another like the opposite ends of a magnet. Fire can't dwell with water, or in the words of someone I know, "Devil can't dwell with God."

One who is in lust will always be wanting more than what one has. *The measure of difference between want and lack of it is depression and pain.*

20

Anger

Anger is never without a reason, but seldom a good one.

~ Benjamin Franklin ~

It is said five minutes of holding on to bitterness wastes more energy than 8 hours of ditch digging. I don't think it is an exact science, but I know my anger drains me. I remember when I threw tantrums as a child, my siblings used to chide and compare me with other hot heads we knew. That infuriated me even further! At first I felt stronger with the rush of adrenaline, but once it was depleted I felt tired and confused; I also had to deal with the consequences of my rage.

Anger leads to depression. In a state of anger you may experience an initial spark of freedom being released from the pressure of frustration. But most of us can testify that experiencing consuming anger is not pleasant. Uncontrolled, it becomes chaos like a dam breaking and letting out water. There are however, two types of anger, one is good and the other is bad.

Anger Is Bad If It Is Out Of:
- Selfishness or self-consciousness.
- A sense of insecurity.
- Shame.
- Pride and self-righteousness.
- A spirit of revenge or murder.

Anger Is Good If It Is in Reaction to Injustice:
Anger is only justifiable if it is accompanied by self-restraint— meaning, if it is a proper reaction, and not an overreaction. Remember, it is not the temptation of the anger, but what you do with it that matters. Anytime self-control is lost anger becomes bad even if it started out well. When controlled with the right attitude, motivation, expression, and action, anger can be good. *Good anger always strengthens one's spirit and clears one's mind.*

Unbalanced Lifestyle

In 1978 a large crowd watched a world renowned 73-year-old tightrope walker Karl Wallenda, one of the great family of Wallendas, walk across a rope tied between two hotel towers in San Juan, Puerto Rico. The dazzled onlookers looked up toward the top of the ten-story building as this legend perfectly handled the balance beam, and slowly made his way across. Karl once said, "Being on the tightrope is living; everything else is waiting." The crowd knew he could do it, because he had achieved the most daring feats many times throughout the decades before. All of a sudden to the horror of the crowd, Karl lost his balance and fell to the pavement below.

Similarly a life that is incorrectly prioritized or wrongly balanced leads to unhappiness. You can desire something, telling yourself that no matter what happens I will achieve this one goal, one thing, above all else. For instance, if you place your job above your marriage or beauty above health, you might be leading a wrongly prioritized lifestyle. Accumulating money is important, but valuing it above your integrity or health is the result of wrong values.

My friend Carl, a successful real estate agent, told me about his mentor, Nate. Nate showed him the ropes and everything about finding right deals. They were best of friends. Then one day the police called Carl to identify a body. Nate was so focused on his desire for success he neglected other important areas such as relationships, health, and proper rest. Focus is important, but Nate took it to the extreme. He wanted success above everything else. Success is good, but like so many people he wrongly thought success (that is commonly accepted as wealth, prestige, or fame) would result in long-term happiness.

Unbalanced areas can be many. As we mentioned previously, proper care of self is good, but excessive care of oneself can lead to selfishness. Confidence is good, but taken to an extreme, it becomes arrogance. Generosity is good but overdoing it results in negligence. I like this passage from Ecclesiastes: "It is good to grasp the one and not let go of the other. The man who fears God will avoid all extremes."

In 2012, the great-grandson of Karl Wallenda, Nik Wallenda, made an attempt to be the first person to walk across a tightrope stretched directly over Niagara Falls from the US to Canada. The feat was broadcast internationally with an estimated one billion viewers and more than 125,000 sightseers at the famous gorge. As he walked, the water 200 ft below him crashed over the precipice at 65 mph. He was buffeted by swirling clouds of spray. But he kept his balance, and after 25 minutes he traversed the 1,800 ft. gap. Immediately after the crossing, he was greeted by a border patrol officer who asked, "Do you have a passport?" The crowd laughed. When interviewed later he told the reporter, "This is what dreams are made of. I hope what I just did inspires people to reach for the skies."

Worry

Do not worry about tomorrow,
for tomorrow will answer to today.

After the White House was built, people from all around the country came to view this new magnificent building. There was one elderly lady who lived in a distant countryside. She had lived on farms since she was born. When she heard about the new White House she wanted to go see it. The city was quite an impressive sight; she spent hours looking around and enjoyed it thoroughly. Then finally she made it to the White House. Standing on its front lawn she admired the beautiful architecture with awe. Now having traveled all day she felt the need to empty her bladder. She looked around but didn't know who to ask. Everybody round about seemed to be busy. So she did the unthinkable in the eyes of the bystanders. She got down and put her skirt over her head where she could see no one, and relieved herself thinking, *it is no one else's business but mine.*

Unlike the lady in the story, we often find ourselves worried about so many things: what people think, what tomorrow will hold, or if we will have enough. Like a wet blanket, stress, worry, and guilt quickly snuff out the happiness that has been lit up inside us. These emotions are all rooted in fear.

Most of pain is not physical but mental and spiritual.
Most of it is from self imagined anticipated pain that is unreal.

Guilt is fear of the past, worry is fear of the future. Both fears rob you of strength and effectiveness in the present—which alone is reality. Fear always triggers our imagination, and whether good or bad it is the nature of imagination to amplify beyond its true size. I see this regularly with my 3-year-old daughter Enaka. I corner her and pretend to tickle her in areas she is most sensitive. I do not even touch her, all she hears is me telling what I am about to do. She immediately starts to giggle, laugh, and becomes hysterical acting as if it is happening. And in her mind it is. You probably experience this too.

When older people were asked what they would do if they had another chance, the typical response was, "I would have more real problems and less imaginary ones." Most fears are imaginary—95 percent of yours don't come to pass. 4 percent happen because of your fear, and you can certainly conquer the remaining tiny 1 percent.

<u>Worry Shows Up in Many Forms</u>
- Anxiety, stress, hopelessness, despair, discouragement, discontentment, or frustration.
- Thoughts go through your mind about the future that *rule* you, *control* you, and leave you feeling helpless.
- Tormenting burden.

Caution is a mental process. Worry is a destructive emotion.

The word *careful* was formed merging words *care* and *full*. The word *care* originally meant "to carry a burden". An adequate load on a ship keeps it afloat and moving, but a full load sinks it. Give *proper emphasis* in all areas of life. *Excessive care* over something or *excessive planning* toward the future leads to worry.

I have met many fierce and mighty worriers in my lifetime, and they were all barely making it through each day. I know, because I was one of them. When I was in grade school in the city of Seattle I delivered our local paper around my neighborhood. I got used to my route and enjoyed doing it. But one thing I couldn't get used to was dogs. It seemed like all the dogs in the world were living on my paper route. And not just ordinary dogs, the biggest ones I had ever seen. Some of them seemed big as houses to me at the time. Every day I had anxiety attacks from needing to face these Godzillas. They seemed to hide, waiting for me to come, then out of nowhere they would jump out at me. I still remember this one instance where a huge German Shepherd ran out of his yard and charged me. Before I could react, he put his front paws on my shoulders and barked right in my face! All the hair on my body stood up. I was terrified. I will never forget it.

You may have heard the saying, "Do not attempt to cross the bridge before you get there." Unfortunately that is what you are attempting to do every time you worry. If you do, you are only dwindling away your life energy in an act of insanity. I see many people procrastinate and worry about having to do what they don't like, i.e. doing taxes. But when you procrastinate, the problem only compounds. If you focus your mind on what you can't control, you are guaranteed to worry and get depressed. *The right way to deal with situations you don't like to deal with* but are necessary to do is to *focus your mind and effort on what you can control and immediately act on it. What you can control is your focus and belief.* As you proactively take care of what you need to do, your worries, will diminish or go away. It is said that Thomas Edison hardly ever got upset in spite of all the failures he faced in his experiments. Never waste energy worrying or getting upset, rather use your energy to find solutions.

Take these steps and eliminate your worries:

1. Find the facts. Get *all* the facts.

An attempt to make a decision without sufficient amount of certainty creates worry.

2. Unearth the *cause* of the problem.
3. Write down your questions and answers to clarify your thinking.
4. Consider the worst possible scenario, and be willing to accept it if it is out of your control.
5. Brainstorm all possible solutions and list them in order.
6. Take massive action and execute those solutions.

TRAP

 If you focus your mind on what you can't control, you are guaranteed to worry and get depressed.

TIP

 Focus your mind and effort on what you can control and immediately act on it. What you can control is your focus and belief.

Guilt

I was heavily involved in my high school tennis team. Being the lead player, I volunteered to speak on behalf of my team in one of the monthly school assemblies. Although I didn't have any experience in public speaking, I said to myself, *I earned my right, I want to make myself known.* So there I was in front of about six hundred students who had gathered in the gym. After the initial introduction about myself and the team, I stepped up to the podium. I didn't practice for my speech. I just figured I'd know what to say when I got up there. When I looked out at all those faces, I froze; my heart pounded faster and faster. I didn't know what to say next. I turned and looked at my teammates. "Uh, Erik, would you take over?" I came down the podium like a dog with its tail between its legs. Let me tell you that was perhaps the most embarrassing experience I ever had. Shortly after that incident and even many years after, a sense of failure and shame associated with that event returned randomly, pricking my mind and emotion as if it were with a pin.

TRAP

 Worry is fear of the future; guilt is fear of the past, or fear regarding the past.

Guilt has its place in us, but excessive guilt called self-condemnation is destructive. Everyone is born with a moral compass called "conscience" which God put in us to distinguish right or wrong in respect to other people and ourselves. The problem is a conscience can be feeble or it can be unenlightened; it can become overly sensitive or overly dull. If seen in a wide spectrum, it would range from weak, defiled, hardened, to seared.

And to an extent it can also be programmed according to the culture you live in.

There are two factors that help determine which part of the conscience range we end up in. One is our personality trait—it prompts us toward one of these points on the spectrum. The other is from choices we make. Every choice we make either puts us closer or away from the healthy state of knowing right from wrong.

Our conscience, then, isn't always reliable, but nevertheless it is the very basis of what makes and keeps us human. Thus, in spite of its imperfections, it must be kept pure, guarded, and carefully adhered to.

Certain habits can lead you to condemnation. Overt analysis and introspection over one or another's actions can easily lead to self-consciousness and condemnation: "Did I do wrong?", "Is this right?", "Why did that person say that to me?", "What does that person think about me?", "Why does that person look at me that way?"

Harboring past failures may result in living ineffectively in the present, or even repeating those failures. Those who are introverts especially need to say NO to the tendency to: overly analyze people's inputs, engage life too seriously, and have a low self-image. Difficulty arises because from a distance, condemnation and conviction look similar. I see many people mistaking condemnation for conviction and vice versa and living in unhappiness. Mistaking the blade of a knife for its handle can result in much harm. Look at the list below and learn to distinguish these feelings. Then resist condemnation but embrace conviction.

Condemnation (excess guilt or shame)
- Gives you a sense of failure.
- Fills you with hopelessness, despair, and depression without solution.
- Makes an embarrassing moment and repeatedly comes back to you even after you've made things right.
- Involves fear, fear results in paralysis and lack of change.
- Exhausts, overwhelms, and makes you feel like you are not going anywhere in life.

Conviction
- Gives a specific clear solution.
- Gives hope and sense of confidence.
- Makes you feel refreshed when you correct a mistake. The error doesn't haunt your memories.
- Keeps you focused in the present (in which you can change the future) and in its reality.
- Doesn't overwhelm you. If you have a thousand things to correct about yourself, it asks you to start with a few of your biggest ones and at a pace you can handle.

Legalism or Lawlessness

In the middle of a weekday evening, a small town in the state of Arkansas held its town meeting. The people in attendance discussed various issues of concern, but there was a topic which everybody waited eagerly to debate. It was whether the town's women should wear makeup or not. The debate continued on for hours. An equal number of people were for and against it. Among those who were against it was the town's historian. He stood up and said,

"As a historian I must tell ya, it was Cleopatra who set the trend of coloring eyelids and painting them nails, and let me tell ya—she was none whom our women ought to follow." Most of the people seemed to nod their heads.

Another person who was against makeup was the town's merchant. He stood up and said, "I am against it because when I traveled to distant cities in Europe I saw prostitutes walking around in the daylight! And they were wearing makeup, and lots of it! Certainly gentlemen, our town's respectable ladies should not be like those prostitutes."   This time most of the people clapped and whistled.

Finally one old farmer stood up and said, "I haven't been educated and don't know much about history. I have been a farmer all my years in this town and haven't seen much of the world. But I know one thing, any barn looks better with a coat of paint on!" The issue was settled.

When you are bound to excessive rules, or fall in the habit of constantly being preoccupied with "ought to", "must", and "will", you are in danger of experiencing depression. In a subtle way you can get burdened by rules, standards, and goals that are put on you by others or are self-imposed. These kinds of regulations can constantly make you feel that you should do or be more, and how you don't measure up.

Even enjoyable activities can lose their luster if they become obligations or requirements. A study was conducted with nursery school children who liked playing with Magic Markers. One group played to win while the other group played for fun. A couple of weeks later the children who'd previously participated to win showed less enthusiasm to handle markers than the children who'd participated for fun.[2]

Goals and resolutions are necessary for motivation and success, but they often put us under the law mentality and burden. Therefore, have goals, but view them as destinations, not as requirements. One well-known shoe advertisement's slogan put it well, "Just do it." Do not say, "I have to", but rather say, "I choose to", "I want to", "I am going to have fun doing this and completely enjoy the process!" *Place joy, not burden, as your life's motivator.*

Lack of proper absolutes also may lead to insecurity and depression. A different study was done on a group of children in a nursery school yard. The theorist thought children would experience more freedom in the absence of a barrier. When the chain-link fence was removed however, the children stayed near the center of the playground. They did not run away, but they stayed away from the edge of the grounds.[3]

There are principles that govern our world. We benefit by adhering to a balanced and healthy set of rules.

Engaging Life Too Seriously

Engaging life too seriously is unhealthy. It can easily put your frame of mind to the law or obligation mentality and leave you with stress and guilt. A place of right balance of serious playfulness keeps us on the edge of maximum productivity.

Seeing and approaching life issues as a game can keep you from being overly serious and from being a slave to your own emotions. It does not mean irresponsibility should be encouraged, it just means you will benefit most by giving each issue its due.

If you take life too seriously, you'll be at war with everyone over every matter. It will build stress, ruin creativity, and sap the joy and strength out of you. A child who doesn't laugh much is an abnormal and sad child. Being too serious is not childlike—children laugh all the time. Laugh through life—laugh as much you possibly can. Children laugh 300 to 400 times a day, but adults only 15 to 20 times a day. Children are much happier and have more fun than adults.

TRAP

 Except for a few things in life don't take things too seriously; if you do, you'll be at war with everyone over every matter.

TIP

 Laugh through life; laugh as much you possibly can.

If you are too serious you will quickly burn yourself out, get discouraged, lose passion, strength, and motivation. However, in the place where you are aptly serious and playful, your passion will continually be lit, your mind will be focused, your creativity will flow, and your strength will endure. When you release your "inner child," the result is greater productivity.

Burnout

I enjoy weight training to stay in shape. I started in my teens and have kept at it into my adult life. By nature I like to push myself to the limit. When I was in college, I used to go to the weight room six days a week for one to two hours each time. I was full of testosterone but empty in wisdom back then, and no one told me how to tell the difference between the good pain verses the bad pain. I had basic training on weight lifting. And from this training two things stayed in my mind, "No pain, no gain" and to stop if it hurt. At first although the pain I felt was rather sharp, I kept on pressing myself, wanting to gain. We do not know our limit until we press toward it. Sometimes consequences are minor, so it is all right. Other times it is not and there is no way to back step for having gone beyond the limit. I felt a sharp pain in my back, and I could barely move. For the next three to five years, I could not sit longer than ten minutes at a time. Those were difficult years for me.

Therapists say only to spend about 70 to 80 percent of your energy so that you will not burn out. This applies mentally and physically. Otherwise it will cause damage, and time spent recovering (if that happens) will take longer than if you did not burn out. This percentage would vary slightly by age since as people get older the recovery rate is slower. People live in two zones: zone of stress or the zone of fulfillment.

Zone of Stress

People who are stressed generally spend less than 25 percent of their time in the Zone of Fulfillment (doing the things that are urgent, but not important), and spend a lot of time in the Area of Demand. They develop an urgency addiction and tend to make things that are not urgent appear important. They are those who get stressed a lot. If you are constantly in the urgency mode it is because you are bound to a To-Do list.

Zone of Fulfillment

If you want to be happy and achieve at a much higher level in life, you must spend an average of 40 to 70 percent of your time in the zone of fulfillment (planning, designing, creating something new, evaluating, improving, keeping the passion lit, finding better opportunities for the company, family, friends, and personal reflection time). Resist the temptation of the Have To mentality. Do not focus on To-Do, or "I don't have the time." Focus rather on results, "I have so much time and so little to do, I can." The fact of the matter is, you don't have to do anything. Tell yourself, "Today I choose to…"

Spending 90 percent in the fulfillment zone will leave you flabby and ineffective. So you want to avoid that as well. Know how to relax and enjoy the process; keep the passion about life, relationships, and your job. You will find you get a lot more done that way. If you are grateful and fulfilled, you are in this zone. Make sure to keep your physical and emotional health optimal before important events, and you will be more productive.

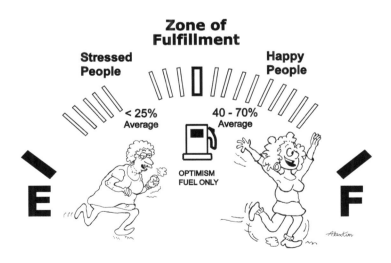

You probably experience this too, when I am fatigued, I am more susceptible to sickness and worry. Prevent fatigue through relaxation and rest before you reach your threshold. I know a former two star general who fought beside General Douglas MacArthur. Today at the age of eighty-two, he exercises in the morning, naps in the afternoon, runs several businesses, swims in the evening, and sleeps five hours over night—daily. During World War II, Winston Churchill worked sixteen hours a day for many years. After lunch, he slept for an hour. In the early evening, he slept two hours before dinner. John D. Rockefeller lived to be ninety-eight and left a legacy of being one of the wealthiest men in history. He had a half-hour nap in his office every noon amidst his busy schedule.

WORLD WAR II — EUROPE.

TIP

Ask and you will receive. If you ask the right questions you will get the right answers. Ask yourself throughout the day, "How can I complete the most important items on the To-Do list and enjoy the process?"

The bottom line is, do the best you can in life without burning out. You probably know this from your experience dealing with cars. If you keep the oil of your car changed regularly, keep it maintained, and avoid stressing the engine—it will take you many places. On the other hand, once you damage the engine by not doing these things, the cost of restoring it to its previous condition may be prohibitive, and there is a chance your vehicle may never run again. Give your body and mind adequate rest and allow full recovery each week. Remember to keep happiness your top priority. If you are driven by work and accomplishments, you'll never reach the end, because there will always be the next goal to reach. Find contentment from within, and go at a pace where you experience overflowing happiness.

PART 1

ATTITUDE IS THE KEY

CHAPTER 4

Happiness Is Relative

Nothing can stop the man with the right mental attitude from achieving his goal; nothing on earth can help the man with the wrong mental attitude.

~ Thomas Jefferson ~

One lovely, sunny day in Colorado, a business man from New York was driving by a beautiful vineyard. He pulled his car over to have a closer look at what was not common scenery in the city. Seeing an old farmer standing looking worried, he went to strike up a conversation and said, "It is a nice sunny day, it must be good for the grapes."

"Yes," the farmer responded, "but it is bad for the carrots." The business man had nothing else to say.

The following day the business man went outside and saw that the day was overcast and dark clouds dominated the sky. Hoping to carry on a better conversation than previously, he walked over to the farmer and said, "It is a nice cool day, it must be good for the carrots."

"Yes," the farmer responded, "but it is bad for the grapes!"

Our world has different seasons and so do our circumstances. Different crops thrive in different climates and so do people. One needs sunshine, another rain; one condition of life will not fit everyone, no more than one suit of apparel will fit everybody. Prosperity is not fit for all, nor adversity.

Life is full of troubles, but we grow through life's challenges. *If life is trouble free we would grow no more than the maturity level of a child.* I have seen many who are physically old, but their mental and emotional maturity level is that of a child. You probably have too.

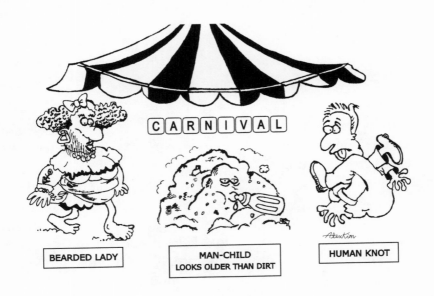

| BEARDED LADY | MAN-CHILD LOOKS OLDER THAN DIRT | HUMAN KNOT |

You can have a good attitude and win in both climates or you can have a bad attitude and lose. It depends on you. Be certain, if you allow circumstances to advise you, you will never be happy.

Our mind works like a camera. In a room there are many colors. If you zoom in the camera toward the color green, you will think that is the predominant color in the room, when in fact it is the least of all colors. Our mind can't discern the truth. I see this through my three-year-old daughter. She would cry in frustration about some little thing, but as soon as I turn on her favorite show her crying stops and she becomes perfectly calm. Previously all she saw was the problem. Then the show took her focus away making it nonexistent in her mind. Whatever the mind focuses on, that is the reality we perceive.

TIP

What you think and speak, is what will grow your faith. Your faith will grow toward that which you focus your senses on. Faith is the substance of things not seen. Faith is seeing as it is, but then better than it is looking into the future. If you want to see a person's past, present, and future, just listen to his or her words.

It takes some time to develop habits that help you see the positive. If you set your mind on the negative or what you fear, you are guaranteed to succumb to these destructive forces. So why not focus on those which empower you? People commit suicide because they have the wrong focus. *What you set your mind on determines how you feel.* In everything, focus on what builds confidence and charges your spirit.

AT LAST, AFTER MANY LIGHT YEARS,
ALIEN SCIENTIST CONCLUDED THAT EARTH WAS SQUARE.

We face reality, and some things are absolutely certain—however, many things can be viewed from one angle or another, negatively or positively. *So if an interpretation can be made over a situation, do it in a way that empowers you.* Dr. Samuel Johnson said, "The habit of looking on the best side of every event is worth more than a thousand pounds a year."

Attitude is one of the most important contributors to happiness. Our minds determine our attitude. We can respond positively or negatively. It's how we react to events, not events themselves that determine how we feel.

During the mid 1990s Microsoft was building the next version of the Windows operating system. I was thrilled to be part of a company that became a household name. Everyday I looked forward to going to work. But the excitement abruptly ended when my position was terminated. I felt like I was hit by a two-by-four. Hopelessness overtook me as I wallowed in pessimism.

Shortly thereafter I was hired on by an internet start-up amidst the dot-com boom. This opportunity seemed even better than Microsoft. Our company was getting rounds of funding, and becoming millionaires seemed inevitable. We knew our company's online shopping platform was going to be Amazon.com's greatest threat. In the spring of 2000, the dot-com bubble burst. My kind hearted manager shed tears for his team, as members were let go, one after another. Although it was difficult, I decided to have a better view of the situation than the last time. As a result, I grieved less and my emotions recovered much quicker. The situation was similar, but my attitude changed. And that brought a totally different outcome. Here is a dictionary's definition of attitude:

Attitude (noun): State or position of the mind and feeling with regard to a situation; a manner of response to a stimulus (as an object, concept, or situation).

THE TRAGEDY FINALLY HAPPENED.
JOEY BECAME SO OPEN-MINDED HIS BRAIN FELL OUT.

Circumstances almost always change when you change.

A positive attitude is one of the character virtues—one can't have a solid character without a positive attitude; it makes the core and one's source of life. It is hard to get depressed when one views situations positively. A negative attitude, on the other hand, poisons both the spirit and body, not only does it weaken, but it also kills. Is it possible for someone to commit suicide with a positive attitude? A negative attitude left unchecked may lead to killing of self and others.

When I think of people who set examples of good attitudes and are inspirations for the rest of us to follow, I can think of a number of people including Theodore Roosevelt, Helen Keller, and Norman Vincent Peale. But one person less known in this category is Young W. Kang.

Young was born in a small rural town in 1944. His father died when he was 13 years old. The following year while he was playing soccer with friends, the ball hit one of his eyes. At first it seemed harmless, but soon he began to lose the vision in that eye. It was unusual, but the impact spread to his other remaining eye.

In 1960, after several unsuccessful surgeries, it was confirmed that Young would never regain his sight. His mother was devastated by the news and died of a stroke within hours of learning of his plight. His 17-year-old sister was then charged with caring for the family. But the stress from the responsibility for herself and her three younger siblings was too great, and sixteen months later, she passed away from undernourishment and exhaustion. In the span of just four years, Young lost his eyesight, his parents, and his sister. Can you imagine the devastation he must have felt as a boy?

As he coped with his grief, Young turned his focus and resolve to his rehabilitation—and refused to accept the tragedies as his fate. He fought against prejudices, discouragements, and all odds. He resolved that no matter what happened, he would turn things around.

He started by learning to read braille. When he did that, he envisioned himself paving the way for the disabled in the academic arena, and he made an unrelenting effort to achieve his vision. Years later, looking back, what he had accomplished was beyond his wildest dreams.

He went through his undergraduate program with honors. In 1976 he earned both a master's degree and a doctorate from the University of Pittsburgh School of Education in Pennsylvania. In 2002, President George W. Bush nominated Young to serve as a policy adviser on the National Council on Disability. He served as a Vice Chairman of the World Committee on Disability.

Wherever he went, Young emphasized the importance of a person's attitude in achieving one's destiny. He said that a child can grumble and say, "My dad is blind so he can't play soccer with me." Or the child can be thankful and say, "My dad is blind, so he can read stories in the dark for me—as a result, I fall asleep well and have creative and lofty dreams." He went on to say, "Consider the word 'NOWHERE'. It can be seen as 'NO WHERE', or 'NOW HERE'. The only difference is just a space. So is the difference between the one who grumbles and sees negatively, and the one who is *thankful and sees positively*. Don't stare too long at a door that is closed, or you'll miss the window that is open."

TIP

 It is hard to get depressed when one views situations positively.

CHAPTER 5

See Your Future Here

*Things turn out best for those who make
the best of the way things turn out.*

When I met Glen and his sister, Mary, they were in their fifties. Glen was living with his wife, who supported them by cleaning houses during the day, then offices at night. She had bags under her eyes from overtime and shift work. Glen was overweight, addicted to smoking and food.

It wasn't always like this. Ten years ago Glen was an owner of a successful real estate brokerage firm, made a multiple six-figure income, and was the talk and envy among those in the business world. Little did he know his accountant and attorney were embezzling his money right under his nose. Almost overnight, he lost most of what he had and became bitter and pessimistic. While his wife toils, he dwindles her hard earned money in frivolous spending, satisfying his addictions, and is just waiting to die.

His sister, Mary, on the other hand, lost her husband through a car accident around the time her brother Glen lost his fortune. It was a devastating blow for her and her two children. At first she had to deal with her grief, but nevertheless, she continued to run their business on her own. A few years later she started a real estate brokerage firm much like what her brother Glen did previously. It was difficult in the beginning. She had to devote much of her waking hours to it. Door knocking and rejection were challenging. But she kept reminding herself of the successful salesman's creed:

"I view every no as simply one step closer to a yes." Today, ten years later, not only is she earning a multiple six figure income, she has been voted as the number one salesperson in her region. She is generous, cheerful, and a pleasant person to be around. I have never seen Mary lose her temper.

TIP

 Remember, you alone can determine how you react.

Here is a classic example of how *attitude is the hinge on which life turns*—either well or sad. Glen and Mary grew up with the same parents and upbringing. Both had similar IQs and abilities. In fact, losing one's spouse is known to be the greatest stress one can experience, even above that of losing a whole lot of money. The major difference between them was their attitude—one was negative and the other positive. While one wasted his decade blaming others and seeing himself as a victim wallowing in depression, the other strengthened herself through faith and having a positive attitude.

From experience I have learned that if I develop a habit of blaming others for how I react, I feel out of control, weak, fearful of what other circumstances may bring, and depressed. When I do not take *full* responsibility over my own reactions, I will never find the root causes and true solutions to my happiness. And problems will only continue to accumulate until these foul emotions explode.

I am not saying we can be completely dead to outer influences. I am also not indicating that we shouldn't change our environment toward freedom. We need to find the source of problems we are faced with and deal with them appropriately, but how I feel predominantly depends on me. When I have a tight rein on myself,

I am free from the fear of getting out of control, and have greater confidence about life.

With a positive attitude, you will see solutions that have always been there. You will become empowered (mentally and physically) and filled with joy. Sadly the opposite is also true.

IF YOU ARE A HAMMER, YOU SEE EVERYTHING AS NAILS.

Just as we become what we eat physically, we become spiritually (mind, emotion, and will) what we put into our minds. One interesting account I came across was that of Charles Givens. He built a multimillion-dollar empire in the late 1980s as a financial strategist and a banker. However, his childhood was rather difficult. His father deserted the family and left them poor.

He then grew up under a mother who was mentally fragile. She abused him verbally and physically. She busted everything in the house that was breakable. In one instance, she threw a two-pound meat cleaver at him. He felt the wind as the knife barely missed his head and wedged itself an inch into the wall.

Struggling under such conditions, he considered himself a loser, and at age sixteen contemplated suicide. Amidst his desperate plight, one morning he began the day by imagining in detail what it would be like if things were all right for a change. Surprisingly the day went well for him. So he started every morning that way, and believed what he visualized. He also found the less he wallowed in self-pity and self-blaming, and *the more he viewed himself as totally responsible for his life, the more control he gained over what he wanted.* What followed were not miracles, but they almost were. Pretty soon his surroundings began to change.[1]

Constantly immerse yourself in the state of exuberant joy and the future you desire—see it, feel it. Why wait? Enjoy it now. *If you don't enjoy your future now, you never will. Because it takes faith* (based on solid facts) *to reach your vision; and faith is the substance of things hoped for, conviction of things not seen.* Do this with goals years ahead as well as those of the day. Begin and end every day by imagining your perfect (but realistic) day in detail; believe it, and expect it. *Expect that perfect day, hour, minute, and second ahead. Whether the day turns out the way you hope isn't as important as the aspiration* (joy, excitement, and motivation toward something great) *and empowerment you experience.*

Despair is utterly useless, never give in to despair. There is nothing to gain by giving into it. To reach your vision takes all the strength you can muster. And it is the joy and passion within you that will give you that sustaining strength. One proverb says, "The spirit of a man can sustain him amidst his bodily sickness, but a broken spirit who can bear?" One of the greatest kings in history habitually said to himself, "Only goodness and mercy will follow me all the days of my life." Such is the mindset of champions.

When the time comes for me to die, then I will die. But while I am alive I am going to live, and live fully; and there is no other way to live fully than this way. I know that if I take care of my attitude, all the rest of life's details will take care of themselves.

Some people say, "Give me fire and I will give you the wood." But before you can succeed greatly you need to have a great faith and attitude.

HOW FIRE WAS FIRST DISCOVERED.

Attitude is not the result of success,
success is the result of attitude.
Attitude sets your future destiny.

Here is a well proven success formula:

Average attitude, average results.
Bad attitude, bad results.
Good attitude, good results.
Great attitude, great results.

Think, believe, and act ordinarily—you will get ordinary results.
Think, believe, and act extraordinarily—you will get extraordinary results.
Two men looked out from prison bars, the one saw mud, the other stars— what do you see?

CHAPTER 6

How to Grow a Rich Attitude

The Lord works from the inside out. The world works from the outside in. The world would take people out of the slums. Christ takes the slums out of people, and then they take themselves out of the slums. The world would mold men by changing their environment. Christ changes men, who then change their environment.

~ Ezra Taft Benson ~

As a service to our community, I used to go to homeless shelters to talk, encourage, and serve food to those who live on the streets. I did this regularly for several years. Believe me it was a depressing and often discouraging environment. Oftentimes they both looked and smelled awful, and were badly in need of a shower and dental care. Some came from other states to look for jobs and not being able to find them, got discouraged, started drinking, and ended up on the streets. Others were there running away from abusive parents. Still others saw no acts of kindness from people, so when pimps gave them companionship, they quickly turned their way. Many were on drugs, and what money they were able to scrape up immediately went toward their addictions.

They all had stories to tell, and I noticed they deeply appreciated sympathy and listening ears. After spending some time with them I learned the key to becoming a professional street vagrant and an expert in being poor:

First, have a bad attitude.
Secondly, blame others for your actions or reactions.
Thirdly, rely on others.

Do these and you are guaranteed to be depressed, miserable, and poor. All of the vagrants I met were pessimistic about life. In their stories I heard them blaming their parents, society, and luck. Their hope was put on people in government offices to solve problems they refused to face. So they became adult children with no parents to take care of them or discipline them, then they turned to the streets.

I met Adrian at a homeless shelter. He was in his early 20s and had recently gotten off the street. It was hard to miss him because he was covered with tattoos from the top of his head down to his legs. He had a troubled childhood and a broken family. I and other friends shared some of the principles that are in this book.

About six months later, Adrian found a job, was going to college, and acquired a car. He showed his driver's license taken two years ago versus the one he'd recently obtained. His countenance was like night and day. He seemed like a different person!

Evil into Good

I remember a story like that of Adrian's, but one that is more grand in scale. I read about a man named Yosef who lived in the Middle East around 1875 BC. Like Adrian, he was born into a dysfunctional family. His mother died when he was a little boy, and he lived with his father and stepbrothers. Yosef was their father's favorite, so his stepbrothers grew jealous, so much so that when Yosef was sixteen, they secretly sold him as a slave to Egypt.

For the next fourteen long years, he experienced much cruelty, hunger, suffering, and injustice. Falsely accused and locked in a dungeon, he had no family, no friends, and no future. In spite of it all, Yosef maintained his integrity. During this time Pharaoh, who was the ruler of Egypt, had a dream. In it he saw seven fat cows, then he saw seven that were deathly pale. This deeply troubled him and he demanded its interpretation. But no one understood what it meant. Finally Yosef gave Pharaoh its meaning. The first seven fat cows spoke of the next seven economically prosperous years. And the following seven was a warning about a famine that would totally devastate much of the world. Astonished at Yosef's wisdom and authority, Pharaoh made him the second most powerful person next to Pharaoh himself and had him plan for the coming years.

THE SEVEN FAT COWS PHARAOH SAW IN HIS DREAM.

When seven years of famine struck after seven prosperous years, a large part of the world came to Pharaoh and Yosef for food—including Yosef's stepbrothers, who had sold him as a slave! Countless people were saved because of Yosef. He even saved and forgave his wicked brothers. He told them, "You meant it for evil, but God meant it for good!" *When the man met his responsibility, the opportunity met the man.*

Law of Priority: If you take care of the most important things and in order, the lesser things will take care of themselves.

What Yosef said is this, "When you maintain a good attitude and do your best with your responsibilities, failures will become stepping stones toward success. *In this sense, everything can be seen as good.*" Yes, what he went through was hell. But if the unfortunate situation didn't happen to Yosef as it did, the great outcome would never have happened: saving the lives of millions—even his very own.

TIP

Seeing everything as good and desirable is of
paramount importance in living happily.

Yosef honored the law of priority. The greatest outcome will
be yours when you honor this law. When it is ignored, however,
you may get what you want, but it will ultimately become
meaningless to you and leave you feeling unhappy: in a financial
analogy, you may gain a penny, but lose a dollar. Faith and attitude
are most important on the priority list. Faith and attitude are
brothers in arms—you cannot have one without the other. Look
how the law of priority works:

Priority Circle

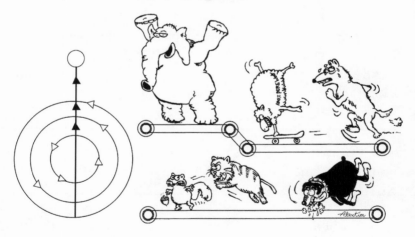

Smaller circles are lesser goals; each exists for the one
immediately above—to help it fulfill its purpose. Also if the goal
is smaller or lower in priority, the more rapidly it changes

compared to the bigger more important goals. Upon every negative circumstance say to yourself, "This (bad situation) will lead to fulfilling higher goals (priorities) reaching all the way to my ultimate goal."

TRAP

 Prejudice is basically mistaking the part as the whole.

TIP

 To see accurately, we must think cubically—see all sides of truth and see them all at once.

I heard a story about a rancher of a country town. One day a fine looking horse walked into his ranch. He looked for the owner but couldn't find him. So he considered it a blessing and kept the horse. Later the horse ran away and was nowhere to be found. So the rancher became sorrowful. But shortly thereafter, that horse brought several wild horses with him. "What a horse of great fortune!" he thought, and gave it to his son as a gift.

The son loved the horse and enjoyed riding it. But he fell from the horse and broke his leg. Seeing his son crippled, the rancher grieved and wanted to blame the horse for the tragedy. That year a war with the neighboring country broke out. All the young men of the town were drafted to war, except for his son. None of those men survived the war. Seeing the final outcome, the rancher was humbled and grateful for this horse, which brought so much blessing to his family.

In our day, we see a similar scenario in the life of Steve Jobs, the co-founder of Apple computer. Unwanted by his biological parents, he was adopted by an average working-class family. At age seventeen he went to college, but seeing how much of a burden the tuition was on his parents and not knowing what he wanted to do in life, he dropped out after six months. No longer bound to program requirements, he freely took the classes he wanted. What interested him was calligraphy. Although there was no foreseeable usage of it in a practical sense, the beauty and artistic sense fascinated him. He couldn't see it then but ten years later, when Macintosh computer was designed, he put what he learned about beautiful typography into its design. He said, "You can't connect the dots looking forward; you can only connect them looking backwards. So you have to trust that the dots will somehow connect in your future."[1]

Never blame or make excuses, but take *full responsibility for your own reactions and actions*. If you don't, while seeing the faults of others, you will fail to see the solution that ultimately lies in you. To illustrate this, picture a woman who may be slipping and about to fall. She would do all she can to stand, grasp whatever she can to find that which will give her traction to stand on her feet.

Having a calm spirit is like this. Your first responsibility before anything else is to maintain your composure—where you are confident, at peace, and sober in spirit—then you will be able to see and aptly deal with others, and not until then.

State of a Healthy Mental and Emotional Equilibrium:
Love, joy, peace, patience, kindness, faithfulness, meekness, self-control, honesty, confidence, hope, faith, freedom, thankfulness, strength, security, clarity, certainty, simplicity, and decisiveness.

When you get upset or have negative emotions that rule over you, your judgments will be clouded and warped. If you act in the state that is out of Equilibrium, you do not solve problems—you waste time, energy, and get nothing out of it but a foul experience. In order to make intelligent and wise decisions, you must be free from such emotions at all times—never be enslaved to them. You can do this by changing how you define reality and looking at what your definition of truth is whenever you face an obstacle:

Truth is found in every thought process that empowers me—that which forms a healthy State of Equilibrium within me. When my emotions are contrary, *most* or the *core* of what I am believing is not real. At the same time, negative emotion is an alert to what is wrong, so don't ignore the problem because it will not go away. Almost always, the *solution* lies in going against my desires and in doing the following: first *act smarter*, second *take the more difficult or longer way*.

The causes of most of our problems are not the problems themselves but our false belief and perspective. So first, to reach the State of Equilibrium, it is important to get out of the warped mindset by recognizing where we are.

Secondly, make it a norm (there are exceptions) to take the more difficult or longer way. Why? Because it is a natural human tendency to swerve toward the way that is easiest; this is where most people fail. So by voluntarily taking the more difficult way we point ourselves toward the direction that is straight and where we truly want to go. And remember, working smart must always precede working hard, because it doesn't matter how hard you work if you are doing it wrong. Do things right the first time.

I am not saying you should think you are superman and can defy gravity, because then you would be standing on slippery ground once again. When your feet slip while walking, the first thing to do is regain your stability. That is what we are after. It is only in the state of mental and emotional clarity and stability that you will be able to assess the situation correctly and make right decisions.

In my professional career I worked with many different people. One memorable co-worker was Tyson Waldo. One week the manager put Tyson to oversee our group meeting during his absence. This went to Tyson's head. There was some conflict with the meeting room reservation where a large group of co-workers were gathered. On many occasions Tyson blew up in anger frustrated with work or against others, but this one occasion superseded them all. For the next twenty minutes a drama unfolded as he slammed the door going in and out of the room, yelling at the top of his lungs and spewing out the worst foul words you can imagine. Later when he came to his senses, he realized what a fool he had made of himself.

Tyson reminded me of David Banner, who, in *The Incredible Hulk* comic book, when he gets angry changes into a monstrous being. When calm, David returns back to his normal self, forgetting what occurred. When people are caught up in their emotions, reasoning gets swept out under them.

Mind, Your Greatest Leverage

PHYSICS DEMONSTRATION DAY

In physics there is the principle of leverage. A lever amplifies an input force to provide a greater output force which is said to provide leverage. Levers can be used to exert a large force over a small distance at one end by exerting only a small force over a greater distance at the other. You can see this in the cartoon above.

Belief → Action → Habit → Result

This is how we function. For best results, leverage your mind—put your greatest effort toward cultivating your mind. *Faith is a by-product of an ordinary habitual thinking process—a process of coming to a conclusion about something as being true.* Whether good or bad, faith and attitude develop from what you focus your mind on. Faith grows based on what you hear. The more you pay attention to something the more your faith grows toward it. One can focus on what is good and be enriched, or focus on the dumps and be trashed. Do you let anyone who knocks on your door enter your house? Don't let every thought that surfaces dwell in your mind. *Monitor every thought—control what goes in* and stays there. You may not prevent a bird from flying over your head, but you can keep it from building a nest there. And be selective in what you read, hear, and watch. The book of Proverbs says, "As a man thinks, so he is."

Control your mind and mouth,
and the control of your life will follow.

Focus on what you want and your faith toward it will solidify. What you consistently (*throughout the day*) *think* about, *believe*, and *speak*, you will be encouraged in that direction. Be your own coach. *Do not listen to yourself, talk to yourself.* Faith comes from hearing, which is why self-talk is so important. Do these consistently, then faith will be there when you need it. Have a regular time where you do these; do them at every opportunity: jogging, swimming, walking, etc. I like the proverb that says, "He who seeks good finds good, but he who seeks evil, evil will come to him." Just make sure that your goals are worthy and noble.

You may be asking at this time, "Are you saying that we should not consider negative issues at all and escape from reality?" No, I am not saying that. Having problems in this world is a norm.

You need to face problems head on by facing reality. This is the view of realists and greatly enhances a healthy attitude. Remember, without problems one would grow no more than the level of a child. Problems challenge our will, engage our minds, and if seen as opportunities, makes us stronger, wiser, and happier. Without them there would be no place for innovative solutions leading toward a better future.

TIP

This is the order in which our spirit (non-physical side) executes:

Mind → Will → Emotion

Information comes to our conscious mind. Then it challenges our will with choices to make. The by-product of the first two steps is emotion—what we feel. For good judgment and emotional outcome, always go in this order. You will *get the best return for your efforts by attending to your conscious thoughts* with utmost care.

To have a positive attitude, engage your mind and conversations on positive things as much as possible. Try to engage 98 percent on positives. If you really have to take in negatives *do no more than where you maintain a healthy State of Mental and Emotional Equilibrium.* Do this to the point where you experience the aspiration toward living, toward your goals, and become empowered.

Upon *every* bad circumstance believe and say, "Thank you for this opportunity." Happy people and successful people *focus on positives and immediately look for solutions. They consider negatives only long enough to identify the problem, then immediately take massive action to look for solutions.* They aptly identify problems and those responsible. Unhappy and insecure people focus on negatives, blaming, and self-pity. That is how typical people react to difficulties. When a negative situation occurs, they focus their minds and words in ways that tear them down.

TIP

Faith comes from hearing, which is why self-talk is most important. Always do it consistently, then it will always be there when you need it.

When I met Henry he was in deep depression. He was a single guy in his mid 20s wanting desperately to get married. He also was stressed to the max from his work. He was a nice guy and felt people were taking advantage of him. He got into the habit of thinking how bad things were all the time. By forming such a habit, he made a groove in his brain like those on record albums. So whenever his mind came to an area of decision, it would get stuck on that track of negativity and play negative thoughts repeatedly. He was hung up on his emotions rather than conquering depression through a right attitude.

AT LAST, DORI SAW WHY HENRY WAS SO NEGATIVE ALL THE TIME.

I suggested to Henry, *"Instead of listening to yourself and what your darkened emotions say to you, talk to yourself.* You can get depressed because a relationship didn't work out, or rejoice because you're a better person as result." I went on to tell him the following so that his mental process would be healthier and more constructive:

- You can complain that your glass is half empty, or be grateful it is half full.

- You can complain for not having hair on your head, or be grateful for having a head.
- You can complain about closed doors, or be grateful for open windows.
- You can complain about having difficulty getting up every morning, or be grateful for life—period.

I encouraged him to ask positive and constructive questions that lead to solutions and thanks, rather than grumbling ones. I had him start with the negatives but end with positives. And I encouraged him to interpret situations positively—in ways that empowered him rather than those that tore him down. I told him to see mistakes as opportunities for growth—to learn and go on. When I saw Henry the next time, he was excited and was doing much better.

Great Attitude Builders

Life changing powerful attitudes can be built by continually focusing on the positives with your mind and words as much as possible:

Not on the bad, but on the good
Not on what I hate, but on what I like
Not on the negative, but on the positive
Not asking negative questions, but asking positive questions
Not on what I can't, but on what I can
Not on what I do not have, but on what I do have
Not on failures, but on successes
Not on improbabilities, but on possibilities and opportunities
Not on problems, but on solutions
Not on deficiencies, but on accomplishments
Not on what isn't working, but on what is
Not on uncertainties, but on what you are absolutely certain of
Not on what you do not know, but what you do know
Not on being understood, but understanding others
Not on minors, but on majors
Not on getting, but giving
Not on do not, but on do
Not on passive, but active
Not on what I can't control, but on what I can
Not on the past, but on the present for the future

PART 2

HAPPINESS IS BUILT ON INTEGRITY

CHAPTER 7

Adamantium Foundation

Righteousness and justice are the
foundations of your throne oh God.

~ Psalms ~

As long as I can remember, I liked comics. When I gathered enough allowance money, I bought one and added it to my collection. One of my favorite comics was the X-Men. With the recent release of movies, the X-Men have become public icons. Two of my favorite characters are Colossus and Wolverine. Colossus is a big man of Russian descent. His advantage is that at a thought he can turn his entire body to metal and become super strong—he also looks really cool. Wolverine, on the other hand, is short in stature. Although not as strong as Colossus he is stocky. He also has a terrible temper—wild and wolf like in instinct. What makes Wolverine so unique is that one, he can heal very quickly from wounds, the other is that his whole skeletal structure is made of the strongest steel known to man. It is called Adamantium and is unbreakable. Attached to part of his skeletal structure are metal claws. They come out at a whim through his knuckles. Because they are so hard, yet sharp, they can cut metal like paper; such is the nature of Adamantium.

Every structure that stands has a foundation. The higher a building rises, the bigger, deeper and firmer its foundation must be. Typical foundations are poured cement, and they must be firm enough to hold the weight of the building as well as resist the force of the wind that blows against the structure above it.

Integrity is the indestructible foundation of a happy person. If you want to build your happiness tower high, do not have just an ordinary type of foundation that can break, have one that is unbreakable—like Adamantium.

The way a single diamond has many sparkling facets, integrity has these: *love, truth, and justice.* A person of integrity lives by the golden rule: "In everything treat others the same way you want them to treat you." Righteousness and happiness are inseparable. You have to be at peace with the law of integrity to experience the inner peace.

Wicked flee when no one pursues,
but the righteous are bold as a lion.

The wicked harm other people—because his defiled conscience torments him, yet he blames others for his own atrocities. Happiness flourishes out of the soil of clear conscience. A person of integrity seeks to suffer, to do what is right, even above having good feelings. Such are the people the world is in dire need of.

TIP

 You cannot change your innate personality with its quirks and flaws, but you can change and grow in character. *Your character is what will lead your personality in a right direction.*

A person of integrity is known distinctly like a lighthouse on a hill by the way he cares for people. He empathizes with others and seeks first to understand, then to be understood. And in humility he places others above himself.

He is as good as his word. When he promises you know he will follow through. He is true to himself and to others.

A person of integrity is responsible. By definition the word responsibility—response-ability—is one's ability to properly respond to a given position. If a father of a family does not play the role to provide or be an example, but rather frequently blames others for his faults or loses his temper—is he a father or is he just a scarecrow? The word responsibility is a foreign word to such a man. As long as you focus on blaming others for how you feel, you will not be able to find the root cause, so a solution is nowhere to be found.

TIP

The force of habit can sway us to failure or to success. The more we do something, the more likely we are to unconsciously and easily do it again. Habit is like a cable—coiled, it binds us as its slave; stretched like a bridge, it enables us to walk across the deepest valley to freedom.

Studies show that it takes twenty-one days of repetition to renew a habit. It takes nine to sixteen times depending upon how much pleasure or pain the habit causes, or upon the individual's unique personality. The point is: *habit forms much of what we call character.*

I heard a funny story about a man who had a fight with his wife. He usually lost when arguments broke out between them. But this one early morning he resolved to prove to himself and to his wife that he was a real man. So after gulping down a whole bottle of whiskey he stood his ground, keeping his pride and chin high as the argument heated up. Outside a cock crowed signaling that it was morning. As the fight escalated the wife chased him with a broomstick to their bedroom. The man hid himself under the bed and would not come out.

"Come out, and face me like a man, you coward!" she cried.

"I will not come out!" the man said as he crawled farther inward under the bed.

"Come out you rat!" she yelled as she shoved the broom stick under the bed as if she was cleaning a chimney.

"I will not come out. When a man makes a promise he keeps his word!" That morning the husband proved his manhood.

When a child of a man of integrity thinks of love, truth, and justice—his father is the first to come to his mind. In dealing with others he practices generosity and seeks win/win: looks for ways where both parties will benefit and come out feeling good about the outcome. He believes that the Creator has given us an abundance of things. God creates everyone to be unique geniuses. It is the greed of men and the *scarcity mentality* that drives much of the cruelty in the world. Do not have the scarcity mentality that says only a few can win and benefit. Think win/win and pursue working with others for the benefit of all. View the problem from various angles and think creatively.

Happiness is the result of having the mentality that sees the abundance given to everyone to share. In such a state of mind, you cannot help but become joyful and generous. The more you give, the more you become successful—it becomes a continuous cycle with a compounding effect enriching all areas of your life. Poverty and a scarcity mentality breed jealousy and discontent, which snuffs out joy and enhances selfishness. Such a mentality causes people to act like crabs. Have you ever caught crabs and put them in a bucket? As soon as one tries to get out the other one pulls it right back in, so they all stay trapped.

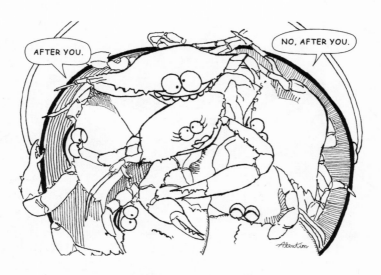

THE DAY MORALITY WAS PUT INTO CRABS.

It doesn't mean you do not compete in a race, become complacent, or irresponsible. It means to compete and work as hard as you can. However, never fall into the scarcity mentality that leads to jealousy. Have this perspective at all times:

- Others may have more money now, but I have what I need [not necessarily what I want] and will rejoice over the abundance which lies ahead.
- Others have intimate companions, but I am blessed with quality people in my life and excited over what the future holds in this area.

- Sue has success but so can John and Jane to their hearts' content.
- I have success now, but there is enough for others in the future as well, and I want to give what I have learned to help them.

One principle that enhances integrity is truly believing that our lives are accountable to the Almighty Creator, who ultimately loves and judges us toward our eternal destiny of life or death, pleasure or pain. In all stages of our lives there are authorities who oversee our actions: parents, teachers, government, etc. Yes, they are imperfect, but in having them we are better off. How well do children behave in a class the moment the teacher steps out of the room?

Many experience joy in God through faith, prayer, and meditation. For decades I pursued spirituality by these means and found comfort. Along my spiritual journey I also saw many pitfalls. I would not accept a belief for the size of its followers or for the length of its existence. In history, nations and empires blindly followed cult leaders, and for the majority of history people believed the earth to be flat. I would not be manipulated into a belief by fear either. Remember, the correct order of spiritual execution is mind, will, then emotion. Often times we can see the spiritual world through the physical world. In the physical world a robber renders the victim helpless so he can steal. Religious robbers attempt to bind people with fear. They try to force people to act in the wrong spiritual order and ensnare them. Process information with apt caution and never give into paralyzing fear that blinds your judgment.

The tree is known by the fruit. Good spirituality is pure, simple, and bears good fruit—mentally, emotionally, and physically. When a particular spirituality becomes complex or leaves you frustrated or fruitless, discard it—even if it might be bundled with other good sources. Test everything. I've seen numerous religious beliefs loaded with idealism and hype that are far from reality. At times what people call personal relationship with God is another form of man-made religion that play on words. Jesus taught that religion should exist for man, not man for religion. What does that mean? It means no claimed divine revelation or tradition should be accepted blindly. Before you get involved in any type of teaching, first see the lives of those who believe them. Observe and analyze to see if the belief agrees with reason and common sense. Then see if it enriches your life. Because we can't see God, your spiritual progress is best known by the measure of your love toward your neighbors whom you can see, as well as a clear conscience and happiness you can feel.

GOD MADE HEAVEN AND EARTH.
THE REST WAS MADE IN CHINA.

Abraham Lincoln's Letter to His Son's Teacher

He will have to learn, I know,
that all men are not just,
all men are not true.

But teach him also that
for every scoundrel there is a hero;
that for every selfish politician,
there is a dedicated leader.

Teach him for every enemy there is a friend,
it will take time, I know.
But teach him if you can,
that a dollar earned is far more valuable than five found.

Teach him to learn to lose,
and also to enjoy winning.

Steer him away from envy,
if you can.
Teach him the secret of quiet laughter.

Let him learn early that the bullies are the easiest to lick.

Teach him, if you can,
the wonder of books.
But also give him quiet time
to ponder the eternal mystery of birds in the sky,
bees in the sun, and the flowers on a green hillside.

In the school teach him
it is far more honorable to fail

than to cheat.

Teach him to have faith
in his own ideas,
even if everyone tells him
they are wrong.

Teach him to be gentle
with gentle people,
and tough with tough.

Try to give my son
the strength not to follow the crowd
when everyone is getting on the band wagon.

Teach him to listen to all men,
but teach him also to filter all he hears on a screen of truth,
and take only the good that comes through.

Teach him if you can,
how to laugh when he is sad.

Teach him there is no shame in tears.

Teach him to scoff at cynics
and to beware of too much sweetness.

Teach him to sell his brawn and brain to the highest bidders
but never to put a price tag on his heart and soul.

Teach him to close his ears to a howling mob
and to stand and fight if he thinks he's right.

Treat him gently,
but do not cuddle him,
because only the test of fire makes fine steels.

Let him have the courage to be impatient,
let him have the patience to be brave.

This is a big order, but see what you can do.
He is such a fine fellow my son.

Thomas Jefferson's Resolution

In matters of principle, stand like a rock; in matters of taste, swim with the current. Give up money, give up fame, give up science, give up the earth itself and all it contains, rather than do an immoral act. And never suppose, that in any possible situation, or under any circumstances, it is best for you to do a dishonorable thing.

He who permits himself to tell a lie once finds it much easier to do it a second and third time, till at length it becomes habitual; he tells a lie without attending to it, and truths without the world believing him. Whenever you are to do a thing, though it can never be known but to yourself, ask yourself how you would act were all the world looking at you, and act accordingly.

LIES, LIES, LIES.
YOUR RESUME FOR THE SALES POSITION IS FULL OF LIES.
GOOD, YOU ARE HIRED!

Helen Keller

The Blind Woman with Vision

Helen Keller was asked, "Who do you think is the most misfortunate person in the world?"

She replied, "One with eyes but without vision."

You probably know the story of Helen Keller. Eighteen months after her birth, she was left completely blind and deaf when she suffered an illness. For five long years she spent her time isolated from the world, alone in complete darkness. It wasn't until a special teacher, Anne Sullivan, came to assist her that she decided to shape her future—one that was bright and full of hope.

"Face your deficiencies and acknowledge them. But do not let them master you," she said.

Helen Keller faced incredible odds, but she didn't give up. She learned to hear and speak through her hands. She graduated from Radcliffe College and went on to take an honored place in society. She stood before kings and queens and presidents. Although tempted to do so she did not give into self-pity. She said, "The marvelous richness of human experience would lose something of rewarding joy if there were no limitations to overcome. The hilltop hour would not be half so wonderful if there were no dark valleys to traverse."

"Character cannot be developed in ease and quiet. Only through experiences of trial and suffering can the soul be strengthened, vision cleared, ambition inspired and success achieved."

The Guy in the glass

by Dale Wimbrow

When you get what you want in your struggle for self,
And the world makes you king for a day,
Just go to the mirror and look at yourself,
And see what that guy has to say.

For it isn't your father, or mother, or wife,
Whose judgment upon you must pass.
The fellow whose verdict counts most in your life
Is the guy staring back from the glass.

He's the fellow to please, never mind all the rest,
For he's with you clear up to the end,
And you've passed your most dangerous, difficult test
If the guy in the glass is your friend.

You may fool the whole world down the pathway of years,
And get pats on the back as you pass,
But your final reward will be heartache and tears
If you've cheated the guy in the glass.

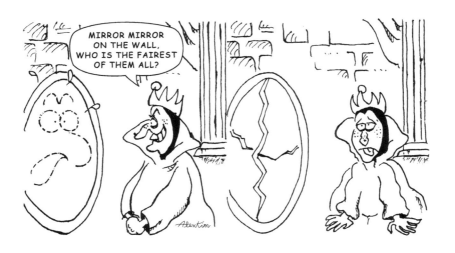

CHAPTER 8

Love and Live

Love is like the light, it is unbending,
but its warmth goes around every corner.

~ Martin Luther ~

During the early 20ᵗʰ Century in India there was a man named Sundar Singh. As a teacher he traveled across many countries and mountains. On one occasion he was going over the Himalayan Mountains with another traveler. As they continued their climb the temperature dropped and snow began to cover their tracks and the area around them.

Hours later they hoped to reach their destination soon, as they were tired and bitterly cold by this time.

"Look, a man!" They came across someone who had fallen in the snow. Quickly Sundar knelt down to see if the man was alive. Indeed he was.

"Let us both carry him with us," said Sundar.

"That is not a good idea. We are both exhausted and in this cold we don't know if we will make it ourselves. We certainly will die if we try to save his life," the fellow traveler replied wiping snow off his bushy beard.

"No, my friend, his life is as precious as ours. I will carry him myself if I have to." Being unable to dissuade Sundar, the fellow traveler went up the hill hurriedly.

Sundar was not a big man by stature; nevertheless, he put the man on his back and started walking with all his might. A mile seemed like an eternity. His legs started to shake and give away. Right then the man he had been carrying came around. His partly frozen body had been warmed by the extra body heat Sundar generated from carrying the man's weight. They were both very glad for having each other and walked side by side. They didn't go far when they saw a man fallen dead in the snow. It was the traveler who went ahead looking after himself alone.

Here is the most powerful definition of love I have come across:

Love is **giving** life to another (happiness) by **sacrificing** one's own (joy, comfort, sense of worth, desire, wealth, strength—even one's very existence), according to **wisdom** out of cheerful **benevolence**.

Generous people are rarely mentally ill people.

Do you want to be happy? *Be conscious of others' needs more than your own. Live for others.* Be generous toward others, praise good works in their lives, and meet their needs. It is love's nature to give, and give extravagantly. *Love is like a fresh river that continually flows.* Selfishness withholds and puts a stop to such a river—like the Dead Sea—nothing can live in it. *Love is the greatest of all good* and selfishness is the opposite of love and the greatest of all evils. *Selfishness sucks life out of your soul the way a leech sucks blood out of a body. Selfishness dampens all good.* What are other opposites of love? It is *hatred*, but also being *indifferent*, a simple neglect. It is being *apathetic, hard hearted, and cynical.* I like this proverb, "There is one who gives generously, *yet* increases all the more, and there is one who withholds what is justly due, *and yet it results* only in want." Many times, *financial poverty is just a manifestation of an inner mental poverty*—false beliefs. Cultivate a right heart and attitude, then combine them with good financial knowledge, and you will experience an abundance of prosperity and happiness.

TIP

 When you experience more happiness in giving than getting, you are experiencing love.

Love gives life because it gladly meets people's basic needs: *value, care, praise, and hope.* At the same time, I realize I can mistakenly go to the extreme of giving, and in doing so, do more harm than good for those I am attempting to serve by spoiling them. Love lives at a right point of balance. I have learned that when I have more joy in giving than getting, I am at a good place. *Love is the greatest thing there is.* And love is the most important source of happiness. Without it, our lives become empty. With it, our lives vibrate with warmth and a sense of destiny. Even in hardship, love shines through. Therefore, I encourage you—pursue perfect love.

Like a precious gem, love is rare. Few people know how to love in its truest sense. Often people misunderstand what love is. Many of the movies and media seem to wrongly convey what love is as well and mistakenly portray lust for love. *Lust blinds.*

"I love you." Few words in the English language are used as often, and at the same time few words are used lightly without substance as often. Therefore, many reach for happiness through what they perceive as love, but it eludes their grasp like the wind.

Happiness is nothing but a by-product of love perfected. When happiness is pursued directly, it is always one step away. Try to love others, and happiness will come to you, and embrace you.

Righteousness and peace have met together,
Love and truth have kissed each other.

~ Psalms ~

Bonnie was in a parked car with her boyfriend Larry. It was a rainy Friday evening at a park in California surrounded by trees blossoming from the spring rain.

"Larry, I like you and all, but I would like us to stay just friends." Those words struck Larry like a jolt of lightening.

"What? I love you. No, I will not accept that!"

With teeth clenched and brows raised Larry quickly turned his face away from Bonnie. It was no surprise to Bonnie that Larry would react this way. It was his idea to celebrate the first anniversary of their dating history. Bonnie's heart started to beat faster and faster. She tried to calm her nerves and said, "I thought a lot about this Larry, and I think it will be for the best."

"Best for whom?" Before he could finish his sentence Larry dashed out the door.

"Larry!"

Bonnie waited hoping that he would return and take her back home soon. It seemed like hours, but it was ten minutes later when Larry returned. He took his driver's seat and sat down huffing and puffing. In the light of the moon, she could see his hand. Something didn't look right.

"Blood…" Then Bonnie realized that while Larry was out he had socked a tree with his hand. Right then, Bonnie knew that Larry was a loser, and that she had done the right thing.

"Date me or I will hurt myself," was what young Larry was saying. He was trying to manipulate and dominate Bonnie's will so he could get what he wanted—whatever that may have been. Larry didn't understand the law of love—*where freedom is chained, love dies*.

Jimmy and Nancy were married for over a decade. When they first met, Jimmy fell head over heels for Nancy. "I will die if you don't marry me," he told her. Initially their marriage seemed like there was a rainbow hanging over them and nothing could go wrong. As the marriage progressed, Nancy began to question Jimmy's sincerity. It felt like the love he expressed before marriage began to diminish. At times she thought he was lying to her. He began going on long distance business trips. Her gut instinct worried her. To overcome her fears, she turned to food for comfort and began to gain weight—a lot of weight. To Jimmy, Nancy began to be high maintenance. When he came home after a hard day of work, all he wanted to do was rest, but she wanted his attention. When his work required him to go out of state to check on the company's plants, he was rather glad. And pretty soon he began a side relationship. Out of suspicion Nancy started snooping through his emails and she uncovered the affair.

"How could you do that to me, you bastard!" But it was too late, Jimmy had already made an arrangement to move away from her. She cried and clawed him, and when that failed, she begged him to come back.

The more she pleaded and expressed how depressed she was without him, the more he distanced himself from her.

"I don't understand why he is running away from me when I tell him I need him—I miss him so much," she told her marriage counselor as she cried.

Nancy didn't understand the nature of love. As we mentioned previously, love does not act to get, it primarily acts to give. It is not self-seeking. The more you try to grab to get, the more love will flee. People who are in a situation like Jimmy feel trapped. So the more they are chased after the more they want to run away.

Love is liberating; it is exhilarating. It is not something that can be forced upon a person. "I have something that will make my people happy," said Pol Pot the communist leader of Cambodia. He then murdered over two million of his people to make them conform to his ideology.

Communism attempts to force everyone to be at the same level in economic and social status—in doing so two hundred fifty million people have been murdered up to this point in history. Advocates of communism say that communism exists to benefit the people, but history reveals that it really is to benefit the few who lust for power. We see a similar folly in the contemporary capitalist countries as well. The abuse is less severe simply because the power is more dispersed among the people.

The best way for our society to help the poor is to teach the basic moral values, and encourage people to voluntarily give themselves to their neighbors for the good of others as well as their own good. I like this poetry from the Bible:

"Love is patient, love is kind, love does not insist on its own way. Love bears all things, believes all things, hopes all things, endures all things. Love never fails."

Where there is love, there is life.
Once we have learned to love,
we will have learned to live.

CHAPTER 9

Dynamite Forgiveness

During his professional baseball career, Jackie Robinson won many honors. He broke into the National League as the Rookie-of-the-Year, won the Most Valuable Player award, and achieved a .311 lifetime batting average. In 1945 he became the first black person to play in the major leagues. But that wasn't his greatest achievement. When he signed to play for the Brooklyn Dodgers, he also agreed with its general manager Branch Rickey that he would never fight, even if others provoked him. Rickey knew many prejudiced ballplayers would make it hard for Robinson and do whatever they could to belittle and discourage him; he wanted to make sure Robinson would be able to withstand the pressure.

"Mr. Rickey," Robinson asked, "you want a coward on your ball team?" Rickey shook his head. "I've got two cheeks; is that it?" Robinson asked. Rickey nodded. When Robinson was harassed verbally or when players slid into base with their spikes high to injure him, Robinson did not retaliate. He turned his cheek the other way and released the steam that built up by working harder to hit or catch better. It does not take a special person to fight back when ridiculed or treated unjustly, but it takes real courage to love and forgive. Jackie Robinson had a heart of forgiveness.

Atomic Bomb of Love

We all face temptations to hold a grudge. Holding a grudge and nursing grievances can affect our physical health as well as mental health, according to a rapidly growing body of research. If you hold a grudge, you give the other person power to hurt you all the more. Once anger and frustration blister in your heart, you will fall farther into the pit of depression. We can't be wounded and expect to go far in life. As long as you hold a grudge against another person, you give them the power to lord it over you and keep you chained in bitterness and depression. You give that person the key to turn you at will—like a puppet.

Total forgiveness happens when the key to your emotion isn't put in the hand of the other person; when you are not swayed by them, but freely love them. It doesn't mean you naively let down your guard. No, make sure you learn your lesson. But don't let your spirit lock up—don't let contention build within you. Don't give into the temptation of taking back your rod of forgiveness; rather immediately bless them—that is, desire the best for them. If it is difficult to do, talk with friends or counselors.

HOW FORGIVENESS DIFFERS BETWEEN CHILDREN AND ADULTS.

Bitterness typically arises out of a lifestyle of selfishness and arrogance. Grace to forgive comes out of a lifestyle of love and humility—you can't expect to forgive someone over an issue unless you regularly give and serve. You will be able to do that much, and no more. If you are offended, empathize and try to understand the act from the perpetrator's point of view. Be altruistic by recalling a time when you were forgiven.

One of the most powerful stories of love and forgiveness took place around 1950 in Korea. Pastor Sohn is called, "The atomic bomb of love" because of his tremendous love toward people. He had served the colony for the lepers, and the Christian church named "The House of Love and Care." His love reached out even toward the enemy who murdered his two boys in 1948. Not only did he forgive the murderer, he adopted the murderer as his son. Shortly after World War II ended, Korea was liberated from the oppression of Japan. But it wasn't long before the communist forces arose in his city and unleashed a disaster. In unspeakable brutality communists killed the police, officials, and all those who opposed their ideology. Sohn's sons became two of their victims.

At the trial of his boys, he saved the youth who killed his children and adopted him as a replacement son. On the day of their funeral, there was a sea of tears in witness to overwhelming love and forgiveness demonstrated by this man whom the town loved so much.

Do it Again

by Alex J. Kim

1. You gave your best but it wasn't enough.
   Give your best again.

2. Caring for people may have left you wounded.
   Care again.

3. What you have built over the years may have turned to ashes overnight.
   Build again.

4. Relationship ties may tear and cause you pain.
   Mend those ties again.

5. Your success may have brought more responsibilities and caused jealousy.
   Still, succeed again.

6. Your biggest dream may have failed to come true.
   Dream big again.

7. Your service to mankind may not have been recognized.
   Serve again.

8. If being honest pushes you toward the back of the line,
   be honest again.

9. If you just made your biggest mistake,
   believe in yourself again.

10. Did you try to love others as yourself and get your teeth knocked out?
Love others as yourself again,
and live with false teeth.

PART 3

BE A WHOLE PERSON

CHAPTER 10

Hey You Good Looking!

Creating an extraordinary quality of life requires a paradigm shift from managing your time to managing your life.

~ Anthony Robbins ~

In 2001, Pixar animation released its fourth film called Monsters Inc. It's a fun movie with unique characters. One of the monster characters is Mike Wazowski. Mike is green with a ball-shaped body, a single big eyeball, and skinny arms and legs. He is oddly shaped but cute. On the screen he's cute, but imagine how you would react if you saw a giant eyeball walking on the street? If we compare our manner of living with an analogy of that of a body, many of us would look like Mike—weird.

There is a story that helps to illustrate this. A wise man and his students sat outside on a lovely day going through their day's lesson. The wise man was explaining how to go through the maze of life and come out the other way safely. Just then they heard a racket—right in front of them four blind men were crossing the street and encountered an elephant. Each stumbled on the elephant and tried to identify what it was.

The first one grabbed the leg and said, "It is a tree trunk."

The second one held the tail and said, "It is a whip."

The third one touched the elephant's trunk. "It is a hose."

The fourth man patted the side of the elephant and was puzzled, but then smiled and said, "It's a wall."

The wise man then turned to the students. "Do you see what happens when you mistake a part to be the whole?" The students nodded. "Understand this principle then, life is like climbing over a mountain, you must *never miss the forest for the trees.*"

To live well it is vital to see life steadily and see it as a whole. But even more importantly, live it as a whole. When you overemphasize one area, you underemphasize another. Research was done in London where a large number of patients' diseases and records were compared for common causes and symptoms.[1] The conclusion was that well over 50 percent of illnesses were caused by "eats too much," "drinks too much," "works too much," "does not get enough sleep," or "is unhappy at home." So many of our problems are due to living in unwholesome ways.

Key to life is to see life steadily and see it whole.

~ Martin L. Jones ~

The world's longest study of physical and mental health has come across a set of factors that individuals can use to determine how well they will age.[2] Since 1937, this study has followed 237 students at Harvard University to find the habits of happy people. Sixty-four years later, the following traits were found to be common among those who lived happily:

1. Interpreted trials creatively and constructively and benefited from them.
2. Regularly exercised.
3. Maintained good health and weight.
4. Had good marriages.
5. Continued to study to improve themselves and their lives.
6. Avoided substance dependence: i.e. tobacco.
7. Controlled use of alcohol.
8. After retirement, stayed creative, did new things, learned how to play again.

Uncontrollable factors that affect successful aging include the parents' social class, family cohesion, longevity of ancestors, and childhood temperament. But we can do something about other factors that are within our realm of control. George Vaillant, professor of psychiatry at Harvard Medical School, who summed up the study said, "Terrible things happen to everyone. You have to keep your sense of humor, give something of yourself to others, make friends who are younger than you, learn new things, and have fun. A successful old age may lie not so much in our stars and genes as in ourselves."

Science has revealed that there are mechanisms in the human body that preserve the extraordinary balance between health and disease. When the balance is shifted, depression and illness occur. Happiness is not in going through a prestigious school, not in one's intelligence, not in being influential, nor is it in possessing a great deal of wealth; rather it is in maintaining one's health (mental and physical), doing good to others, and living in a wholesome way. Here are the key areas of life from most important to least important:

1. Health (mental, emotional, physical)
2. Education and wisdom (knowledge lived)
3. Relationships (family, friends)
4. Job and finance
5. Social and political issues
6. Leisure

Don't be, "All work and no play"; celebrate your special occasions. Be loving, grateful, flexible, disciplined, romantic, playful, focused, passionate, strong, smart, cheerful, giving, and outrageous; be an example of all the good that's possible in people's lives.

Healthy Body Means Healthy Spirit

There is an immediate connection between spirit and the physical body. The state of your mind and emotion has a direct effect on your body, but your body also affects your mind and emotion. More often than not, the impact ratio the mind has toward the body is much greater than the impact ratio the body has toward the mind. Bob Knight, an Olympic basketball coach said, "Mental toughness is to the physical body as four is to one."[3]

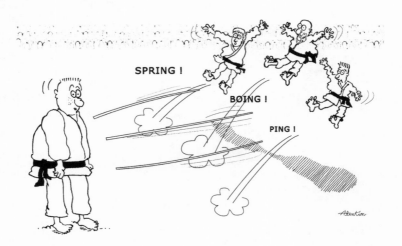

A woman was seeing a psychologist for a long time but was not being cured of her depression. She was intensely unhappy. Another physician diagnosed her condition as a form of anemia. His treatment soon put that woman right.[4]

While in college I injured my back. For several years, it was so painful I couldn't sit down for more than ten minutes. During that time, life seemed gloomy.

No one feels good when sick—confidence diminishes, hormones that enhance good feelings like serotonin and endorphins diminish; even cherished treats do not taste good. Happy people know their body is the horse on which they ride toward fulfilled living; it is the skeletal structure on which other activities are built, so they make it their daily priority.

High levels of sodium can cause high blood pressure, adding stress to arteries. Two other little known factors that damage the heart are anger and stress; of the two, anger is greater. In fact among negative emotions, anger does the greatest damage to the heart. Anger adds stress to the heart by increasing the heart rate and blood pressure. Over time turbulence of blood flow through the coronary artery can cause micro tears and development of plaque.[5]

Harvard Medical School research shows that for those who already had heart disease, being angry more than doubled the risk of cardiac arrest.

Scientific evidence shows that mental and emotional stress adds a great weight to sickness and the rate of recovery. Psychologist Bruce McEwen noticed many different types of adverse effects from anxiety: weakening of the immune system makes us vulnerable to viral infections, colds, flu, and cancer. If someone has diabetes or asthma, stress can worsen those conditions. Stress can also lead to heart disease, stomach ulcers, bowel disease, arthritis, or even loss of memory.

When someone is angry or stressed, depression results. Although the body doesn't seem to be as directly affected by depression, it can noticeably worsen heart disease and the recovery rate. Optimistic patients recover much faster than pessimistic patients, and with fewer medical complications during and after surgery.

IN DESPERATION TO HELP THEIR TODDLER,
THE WALAWALAS SOUGHT TO APPEASE THE POO GODS.

Prevention is the Most Exotic Supplement You Can Buy

By the time a serious illness happens, it is usually too late. Damage has already been done to your body. Everyday we face uncertainties. Risk management is an essential element of living well and reaching our goals.

Sound prevention is nothing but managing risks well. It may have an appearance of fear, but it is different from it. The journey of life may be compared to a ship that moves through treacherous waters with rocks and pounding waves. Troubles come; left alone they may dash you toward these rocks. Prevention is like a ship's steering wheel, and having a map in your hands so you can safely reach the shore.

122

Take a good dosage of prevention, as you would health supplements, and you can well avoid medicine and painful surgeries.

Listen to Your Body

Maintaining optimal physical health is a high priority among those who live happily. They receive appropriate care from the professionals, yet they do not become dependent on them. You are your best physician; no one can know yourself better than you—how you think, feel, and act. No one can properly eat or exercise on your behalf.

Understand what your body is saying to you through its symptoms and conditions; respect your body, do not ignore, listen to it. Know the state of your mental and emotional health through your body also. No one can do these for you nor as well as you can. When your body is healthy, you feel stronger inside and become more capable to handle mental and emotional situations. You are your body.

Have a balanced diet, sleep between seven and nine hours each night, have one complete rest day each week, and get enough sunshine. Exercise is also important. At minimum, walk five times a week, thirty-minutes each time. Do body strengthening exercises (i.e. weight lifting) several times a week. You can maintain your good health this way. Exercise makes your brain release more endorphins, which makes you happier.

Rise in Use of Antidepressant Drugs

In the late 1990s internet usage exploded and so did internet dating. Being single at the time, I checked out one of the bigger online dating services and got matched up with a girl in her twenties named Jill. She was nice, witty, and fun to be around. Over the following months, we got to know more about each other. What surprised me was when I found out she was on an anti-depression drug. I don't think I'd met anyone who was on that type of a drug up to that point in my life. In fact, growing up I don't remember knowing such medications even existed. Since then I've come across other friends, co-workers, acquaintances, both close and not, who either were already on this type of prescription or were starting to go on it. I kept coming across more occurrences at a faster rate. Someone I know said they know so many people on depression medication, it almost seems abnormal if someone is not on it! Some people complain that antidepressants are being handed out like candy and that adults are quickly snatching them like children.

If it is right to use insulin in replacement therapy for the pancreas, there is nothing wrong with taking tablets which influence for good the chemistry of the brain. Mental illness has an "organic" basis. It is something that can be explained chemically.

Drugs seem to help with depression for certain people, especially for those who are in chronic situations. Irving Kirsch, the associate director of the Placebo Studies Program at Harvard Medical School, confirms this by his research as well. However, except for very extreme levels of depression, sugar pills had the same effect as antidepressants. He said, "The difference between the effect of a placebo and the effect of an antidepressant is minimal for most people. If they were mildly or moderately depressed, you don't see any real difference at all."

Most of us probably realize our current society is too quick to turn to drugs for solutions. The problem occurs when people take shortcuts for immediate comfort, even if the solution is only temporary and the consequences grave in the long term. Too often we attempt to deal with surface issues in our lives and do not work toward solving root problems.

One doctor who specializes in depression said that prescribing depression medication has become a regular procedure to satisfy the demands of insurance companies, because it solves the immediate problem and lowers the cost of their coverage, compared to other methods, like counseling. He pointed out that money has been given precedence over human lives. Another doctor said it is a temptation for physicians to want to do surgery or use drugs, so they feel like they are doing the real doctor's work.

It isn't surprising then that at times physicians seem to be quick to offer surgery or drugs.

When I was in my twenties, I went to see a doctor for a physical checkup. During that time, I was feeling unhappy. I mentioned this to my physician, who seemed rather young to me—in his late thirties. He asked me some questions and told me that I was physically fine. Antidepressant drugs were available but he thought I was probably just under challenged in my current occupation. I thought he was right on, and felt liberated shortly after that.

As I have mentioned before, there is a place for chemical therapy. But it is important to have a long term perspective and think about the advantages and disadvantages. It is also important to treat the whole person and not just a part. When I think about the current spike in drug usage, I see the imagery of fire and smoke: where there is smoke there is fire underneath. Fire in our life needs to be put out; just fanning the smoke may only spread the problem further.

CHAPTER 11

Walk Perfectly Balanced

Truth lies in between both extremes.

Remember the story of the world renowned tightrope walkers, the Wallendas in an earlier chapter? Life is like walking on a tightrope. In every area we face, we can fall to either side. The nature of lies keep us in bondage, while the nature of truth sets us free. Truth is found in-between both extremes of life.

One person said there is no straight line in the natural world; that the only straight line is manmade. The most natural thing for people to do is walk, but how many of us walk perfectly straight? When we walk, we shift left or right with each step we take.

The right center of balance is hard to find, but find it we must. For example, confidence is good, but taken to the extreme one becomes arrogant, or even haughty. Planning for the future is good but going too far ahead results in worry and stress. Working hard is good but overwork results in burnout. It is when our lives are correctly prioritized and balanced that we experience happiness.

Life exists on the edge of pushing ourselves toward our limit. I said toward, not over. You don't want to go over. We are happy when we are using our potential. Striving against difficulties and overcoming them—reaching for achievements and finding them—this is happiness. We are happy when we are learning, *growing*, and accomplishing. A tree that is alive grows. When it stops growing it dies. So do people. Working toward a worthy goal that demands our best is an important facet of happiness.

TIP

 A proper state of balance is where self-control is always on the throne.

The following list shows examples where balance is needed in all our lives. I find the major reason for losing my balance is lack of self-control. *And the farther I am away from the point of balance, the more difficult it gets to return.* For example, if I have difficulty going from being confident to being humble, then I have gone to the side of being overconfident or proud. *The right point of balance is where inspiration, motivation, and inner power are sustained and grow.*

Balance Scale

Extreme Left	Truth	Extreme Right
Live in the past	← Truth →	Live in the future
Too open minded	← Truth →	Too close minded
Lawlessness	← Truth →	Legalism
All my fault	← Truth →	All his fault
Careless	← Truth →	Overly cautious
Enjoy only	← Truth →	Accomplish only
All my responsibility	← Truth →	All God or fate
Overly merciful	← Truth →	Coldhearted
Self-abasement	← Truth →	Arrogance
Fall behind	← Truth →	Run ahead
Too relaxed	← Truth →	Strive too hard
Praise too much	← Truth →	Too critical
Too Satisfied	← Truth →	Discontent
Tolerate all	← Truth →	Intolerant toward all
Dependent	← Truth →	Independent
Emotionalism	← Truth →	Stoicism
Sensuality	← Truth →	Asceticism
Fear of people	← Truth →	Oblivious to people
Too generous	← Truth →	Stingy
Do not plan	← Truth →	Worry

PART 4

HAVE CORRECT VALUES

CHAPTER 12

Value Principle

If there is light in the soul, there will be beauty in the person. If there is beauty in the person, there will be harmony in the house. If there is harmony in the house, there will be order in the nation. If there is order in the nation, there will be peace in the world.

~ Chinese Proverb ~

It was a lovely fall evening. The cold temperature had the Berg family starting the fire in the fireplace. Mary Berg and the three children were enjoying relaxing after dinner and anticipating an eventful evening.

"Daddy's home!"

Mom and all the children rushed out to greet their father who had just returned from playing in a national golf tournament with a special guest, Tiger Woods.

"Did you do it Daddy? Did you win?"

"What do you think?" Phil Berg's face shined with glee as he showed his trophy to his family.

"Can I see, Daddy? Can I?" the oldest son, Bobby, asked.

"Okay, but be careful now; it is signed by none other than Tiger Woods himself." Bobby held it tight to make sure he didn't drop Daddy's prize winning trophy. But in his great excitement, he held it wrong. Snap! The tip of the trophy broke in Bobby's hand. "Bobby! I told you to be careful. Go to your room!"

"But, but, but..."

"Now!"

Shedding tears Bobby went. Slam!

"Honey, you should not have treated Bobby that way. It was an accident," Mary told her husband.

"I don't care, that was my prize winning trophy." Feeling guilty about his overreaction, Phil walked away.

The rest of the night was quiet. The evening didn't quite turn out as they had hoped. Who were they to blame? It didn't matter, they retired and were quickly fast asleep while logs crackled in the fireplace. The whole neighborhood turned dark as one by one each of the houses turned off their lights. Hidden by the clouds that danced in the sky, even the moon seemed to have turned off its light this evening.

"Fire!" A voice cried in the street. Mary and Phil woke up to find their house filled with smoke.

"The children!" Quickly they rushed toward their children's room, coughing as they went, barely able to see through the thick dark smoke.

"Mary, quickly get them out through the window! I will get Bobby." Phil rushed to Bobby's room. "Bobby! Where are you?" The room was empty. He could barely breathe. For a moment he thought he was going to pass out. He found himself surrounded by the flames. He looked around the house for his eldest son. Guilt gnawed at his conscience from his earlier words to his son. "Bobby!" Right then his heart sank. There he lay on the floor in Phil's trophy room. In his hand was the damaged trophy. *Is he alive?* As he picked up Bobby, the trophy fell from his hand.

"Dad, I am so sorry about the trophy, I wanted to save it from the fire..."

Outside neighbors crowded around the scene and the sound of the fire truck resonated in the air. "Is everybody out?" the fire chief asked.

"Yes, except for two ... fire has spread too much for anyone to go in at this point."

"We'll give it everything we've got and get it under control!" As firemen hustled, the measure of darkness over Mary Berg's mind was greater than the thick dark smoke coming out of their house. She groped for hope as she held her two children close to her.

Right then she heard someone yell, "There! Look over there!" Overcome with excitement Mary cupped her face in her hands and wept. Phil limped out of the carnage carrying their boy Bobby in his arms.

Their lovely house turned to ashes that night and so did Phil's trophy. But out of the ashes came an important reminder about what really mattered—that his greatest trophy was not what was now smoldering among the ashes, but his boy Bobby—who was sleeping safely in his arms.

Have right priorities and Wisdom will be your friend.

You and I can probably identify with the Berg family in that often times we go through our day-to-day lives in haste, not understanding what really matters. It is when difficulties arise and the heat gets turned on that our beliefs get shaken and readjusted. A house that is built on a wrong foundation will eventually fall when winds or storms blow against it. In the same manner, it is only when our values are properly laid out that happiness becomes our lot.

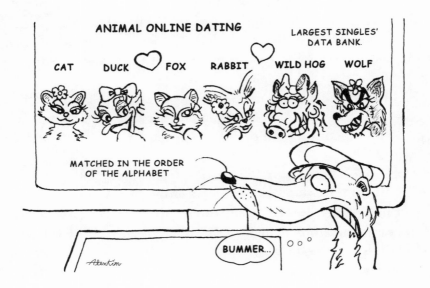

Let us remind ourselves again about the law of priority: *if you take care of the most important things and in order, the lesser things will take care of themselves.* I remember reading how, except for urgent notices, Napoleon used to leave his mail untouched for a few weeks—after that time most problems took care of themselves.

If you are constantly maxed out with your schedule, stressed, and burned-out, then give yourself some extra time—to work like shock absorbers or like a bumper in front of your car. If you overdraw yourself, then you will eventually become bankrupt: mentally, emotionally, or physically.

CHAPTER 13

Desire Right Things

The quality of one's life is the quality of
one's belief and objects of affection.

In the Northern part of the United States, in the deep woods, an exploration team came across an old mining area and what looked like an uninhabited cabin. Within the cabin there lay two skulls and a whole lot of gold. "Why would they have died with a lot of gold?" questioned one of its team members. Combining their knowledge of the area, they concluded, "They probably were so overly excited about the gold, they forgot that in this region winter comes early and hard. They should have taken the little gold they could carry and hurried down the mountain. When the snowstorm hit, however, their food ran out. At that point gold was of no use to them."

Can money buy happiness? The answer is, yes it can—to an extent. But why do people strive to make more when making above what meets our basic needs doesn't really bring additional happiness? Part of it is about keeping up with those around us. We can be millionaires, or even billionaires, but if the Joneses have more we feel we need more too. Once our basic needs are met, socio-economic status doesn't really contribute to one's happiness. And this is the reason why:

"He who is driven by money will not be satisfied with money, nor he who lusts for great riches. This lust results in nothing but depression. Because *when wealth increases, the measure of greed also increases. So inner pain and turmoil remain.*"   (Italics mine.)

~ Ecclesiastes ~

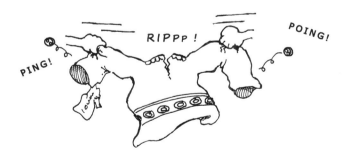

If it is not *money* that people put on their pedestal, then it is either *sex, power, prestige, influence, or materialism*—or even relationships. *There is a limit to the measure of pleasure one can experience before the senses get dull*—the point where the universal law has been set, "This far and no more." Yet people who give into insatiable desire for any one of these reasons are pursuing the wrong goal. *Lust blinds.* That is why we see in the headlines those among the super-rich who, although they have much, still commit fraud and embezzlement.

Better is a dish of vegetables where love is than
    a fattened ox served with hatred.
Better to be a happy preschool teacher than
    an Ivy League professor with emotional problems.
Better to be an honest district major than
    a lying national politician.

Those who constantly seek *great thrills* are never satisfied. Countless have tried to break this rule to their dismay. Even the richest man in history; a man who lived in the Middle East around 950 BC, tried to please his senses in every way a man in his lifetime could try, and at last said that it was "empty" and "unsatisfying". Those who ignore such advice end up with broken marriages, in illegal activities, or they get themselves into many painful situations.

CHAPTER 14

Live Free

In the movie Lord of the Rings, one of the main characters was Gollum. He was once an ordinary Hobbit who became a fiendish figure corrupted by his lust for the power given by a ring worn on his finger. The more he gave into the luring power of the ring, the more gaunt and hideous he became. Gollum developed love and hatred toward the ring, just as he loved and hated himself for being enslaved to it. Lust for power drove him mad and made him like Jekyll and Hyde. One moment he was fine, then another moment he was driven mad lusting for the ring and its power—even to the point of killing. He would often cry out, "We wants it, we needs it. Must have the precious." In the end it was the very ring he sought that killed him.

There is a Gollum in every one of us that keeps us in bondage and weighs us down. A ship that is overloaded will eventually sink. Keep your soul afloat on the sea of joy—be free from greed, worry, and lusts of every kind.

He who masters his passions is a king even while in chains.
He who is ruled by his passions is a slave even while sitting
on a throne.

THE TAMING OF THE SELF

Bondage results in pain and depression, but liberty gives comfort and joy. Slavery is so evil because it results in death—suffering and pain are death. You will experience them if your mind and emotions are enslaved by fear and worry.

Lie   →   Bondage (Slavery)   → Death

Truth   →   Freedom   → Life

Conquer yourself and reign over your
kingdom of liberty and happiness.

Our decision making faculties are our mind and emotions. Both are needed for making good decisions: rational thinking and intuition. However, people naturally are ruled more by extreme emotions than by their minds. Self-control keeps you at a proper balance. It benefits you with a clear mind so you can make right decisions. It is also vital for maintaining a high confidence level.

Self-control breeds self-respect and confidence, which results in success and happiness.

I would like to also mention that many times, we do not pay enough attention to our *silent and seemingly unimportant thoughts*. It is not what we say out loud that determines our lives. *It is what we whisper to ourselves that has the most power.* Self-talk has a powerful effect on your soul.

TIP

 Words form thoughts, thoughts form faith, and faith is what connects you and takes you from the plane that doesn't exist to that which is real. If you want to change your external reality, you need to first change your internal reality, starting mainly with your thoughts.

The main trouble in this whole matter of depression is this: we allow our inner voice to do all the talking instead of letting our self do the talking. Your thought or emotion is often far more powerful in its effect than the voice you hear audibly. Be *alert* and *challenge* it whenever that negative subtle inner voice raises its ugly head and fills you with a sense of inadequacy or self-doubt. *Continue* to challenge self-limiting thoughts and feelings. Say out loud to yourself:

I can do this!
I am *better* than I think I am.
I am *stronger* than I think I am.
I am *more able* than I give myself credit for.

TIP

 Spend more time talking to yourself rather than listening to yourself.

Japanese Seer

During the 18th Century in Japan, there was a man in his late teens who was distressed. He was most dissatisfied with himself. After stirring up trouble in his town, he was imprisoned for a short period.

While in prison, he had nothing to do, so he began looking around at the other prisoners—one after another. In the midst of his exploration, he realized that the countenances of some prisoners were quite different from others. He also began to reflect on his own life.

When he got out, he went to see a monk who was known as the wise man in the city. The monk saw him and told him that if he continued on his current path, within one year he would not only commit murder but would also lose his life.

The monk suggested that for one year he stay away from liquor, women, and gambling, and discipline himself by totally devoting himself to a simple lifestyle and basic foods. Scared out of his wits, the man promised to follow the monk's advice.

His new lifestyle was not easy. It felt like the most difficult thing he'd ever done, but every time he was tempted to go back to his old way of living, he reminded himself of the monk's warning. At the end of the one year mark, he went back to the monk to share his success with great excitement. At first the monk hardly recognized him—he was completely a different man.

Now at this point the man grew curious. Why did certain people turn out well and live happily while others didn't? He kept thinking about the faces he'd seen in prison. They looked so different from those who were outstanding citizens. Unable to find the answer within himself, he decided to make it his goal to find out why.

He started by working at a bath house. There he saw people of every background, age, and social status. He listened to their stories, observed their countenances, and talked to them. Then he researched and discussed his goal with a number of other people. After many years, he concluded that the *key determining factor of happiness or sadness, success or failure in one's life was none other than the degree of control one had over oneself.*

After publishing a book on his findings, letters began pouring in with comments on how much it had helped them. People also had further questions; here are a couple of examples:

Question:
"Others have told me that I am very talented and I see that as well, but I am not going anywhere in life. How can I be successful?"

Answer:
"You are gifted indeed, and have many talents, but this you lack—discipline and self-control. If you master yourself, you will master your destiny."

Question (another asked):
"I have been most fascinated with your book and findings. So I have devoted myself to your teaching and have been doing the best I can to apply it. But why is it that I am still not successful?"

Answer:
"You are on a right path; you will be great and find what you are looking for. But you must be patient and continue in it. For you, success will happen; wait, it is only a matter of time."

Marshmallow Study

Two hundred years later on the other side of the world there was a group of inquisitive minds who made similar discoveries about the importance of self-discipline.

During the 1960s a study was initiated by the psychologist Walter Mischel on the Stanford University campus.[1] Four-year-olds were gathered in a room with one marshmallow placed on each of the children's desk. They were told that whoever waited until the teacher returned before eating their marshmallow would be given two. Otherwise, only one would be given.

As you can imagine, these poor little souls had a huge war going on within as they battled their desire to delay their immediate pleasures for a greater reward. The cutest drama unfolded with a hidden camera rolling.

To help ease their struggles, they covered their eyes, looked away, sang, or even tried to sleep. Others who were more impulsive immediately grabbed their marshmallows as soon as the teacher left the room.

A decade later these children were contacted. Now adolescents, the outcome was dramatic between those who exercised self-restraint at the age of four and those who immediately gave into their impulses. Those who resisted temptation at four were more confident, socially competent, able to cope with stress, responsible, and had endurance under both mental and physical pressure. And they were still able to distinctly delay their immediate rewards in pursuit of higher and long-term goals.

These separate groups distinguished themselves further when they were evaluated again as they were graduating from high school. Those who restrained themselves did far better academically than those who had given in to their impulses; their SAT scores were much higher. They also did better in later years whether solving math problems, playing sports, building a business, or raising a family. The conclusion was that a *powerful vision combined with the ability to control oneself determine an individual's destiny.*

MANY YEARS LATER SUSIE'S LOVE-HATE RELATIONSHIP WITH MARSHMALLOWS WAS FINALLY EXPOSED.

TIP

Discipline is the habit of taking consistent action until one can perform with unconscious competence. Discipline weighs ounces but regret weighs tons.

PART 5

DEVELOP QUALITY RELATIONSHIPS

CHAPTER 15

Life is a Team Sport

Two are better than one because they have a good
return for their labor. For if either of them falls,
the one will lift up his companion.

Gale Sayers, the Chicago Bears' star running back, suffered a serious injury when a tackler collided with him. The situation was so grim Sayers wondered if he would ever play professional football again. What followed were many rounds of painful surgeries and the long road to recovery.

One year later, at the banquet of the Professional Football Writers of America, Sayers stood to accept the award for The Most Courageous Player in Football. The audience was eager to hear how Sayers was able to overcome his setback and make it back to his profession. Many in such a situation would have been glad to tell of their personal achievements. However, Sayers spoke to the audience about another football player who faced even more difficult odds than the severe knee injury that he had to face.

He turned the attention of the audience that night in Chicago to Brian Piccolo. His good friend Piccolo was fighting cancer.

"It is something special to do a job that many people say can't be done," said Sayers. "Maybe that's how courage is spelled out, at least in my case. My teammate, roommate, and friend, Brian Piccolo, kept after me. Brian kept urging me on, sometimes kindly, sometimes unkindly, to fight my way back. Brian Piccolo has the sheer, solid, raw courage which entitles him to win over a sickness that makes my knee injury seem unimportant."

That night Sayers accepted the award, but he didn't do it for himself; he did it for his friend, fellow player, and the source of his inspiration, Brian Piccolo.

"You flatter me by giving me this award, but I tell you here and now that I accept it for Brian Piccolo. Brian Piccolo is the man of courage who should receive the George S. Halas Award. It is mine tonight, it is Brian Piccolo's tomorrow."

"I love Brian Piccolo and I'd like all of you to love him too," Sayers continued. "Tonight when you get down on your knees, please ask God to love Brian Piccolo too."

Under the lights of the stadium one thousand wet eyes blinked. Then there were sounds of cheers and a standing ovation from a crowd which included 24 of the 26 head coaches in pro football. They witnessed how the true stature of a man is not the size of his physique, but the size of the inner man himself. Today they saw the true size of the man Gale Sayers.

In the following years Sayers became one of the greatest running backs in the history of the National Football League. What of Piccolo? Brian Piccolo died of cancer. Together, they showed the world how high human courage can climb when it stands on the shoulders of good friends.

Happy people have meaningful relationships. They have close family and friends with whom they share love and life. However, studies show that quality relationships are becoming less common, and with it, a rise in depression among people.

One *Time Magazine* cover has a picture of a lady looking rather gloomy; and in large letters it says, "20th Century Blues." The article inside mentions how depression levels have increased among the first world countries compared to the third world countries. The more advanced societies also have higher suicide rates. In fact suicide is something that is a foreign concept among the people who live away from the civilized world—like those who live in the jungles of the Amazon. Although people in these remote jungles possess bare necessities and live from day to day for food, they experience close community. They live each day without worrying too much about the future. The closer people are to cities, the higher the levels of depression. High levels of stress and isolated lives have been named as two of the main reasons.[1]

A study done over twenty years involving over thirty thousand people shows that social isolation doubles the chances of sickness or death. Studies show that isolation itself can reduce one's life expectancy as much as smoking, high blood pressure, high cholesterol, and obesity. Smoking increases mortality risk by a factor of 1.6 percent, whole social isolation by a factor of 2.0 percent.[2]

When we look at both historic and recent cases of massacres, they have one thing in common. Killers had very little social interaction—they were isolated and did not have close meaningful relationships. People are social creatures. We are not meant to live alone. Happiness exists amidst love shared in close relationships. However, in families, where this should be seen first and foremost it has been found wanting. Family breakups and divorce rates have been rising. Also, in our fast pace and technology driven age, it has become more difficult to develop close relationships.

Our job climate puts another obstacle in the way of quality relationship development. People stay fewer years in the same company than they did 30 or 50 years ago. It makes it hard not only for us to build ties with others but also for children as they have to move more frequently. People with inner turmoil have difficulty not only having close relationships but also keeping them. This breeds a constant sense of loneliness within.

So develop meaningful ties—mend them as you go along; nurture them and watch them flourish like lovely palm trees in your lives.

CHAPTER 16

Surround Yourself with Happy People

He who walks with wise men will be wise,
but the companion of fools suffers harm.

Once there was a boy with an insatiable curiosity. He was curious about things in the sky above, things that crawled on the ground—he was curious about everything, why and how things worked as they did.

He asked his mother why geese sat on their eggs. His mother said, "To hatch the eggs." One day his parents looked for him, but he was nowhere to be found. After searching around the house, they looked outside. There he was in their neighbor's yard, sitting patiently on a batch of geese eggs, trying to hatch them.

When he was put in school, he had so many questions the teacher thought he had a learning problem. So finally his parents took him out of the school and taught him at home. He only went to school for three months his whole life. In spite of what others said or how they laughed behind their backs about the child, his parents believed in him and gave him hope and encouragement. Surrounded with people who cared, he continued in the direction his natural curiosity took him. Years later he invented the electric light bulb, phonograph, motion pictures, and filed 1,093 other patents. His name was Thomas Alva Edison.

WHAT WOULD HAVE HAPPENED IF THOMAS EDISON'S
PARENTS HAD NOT BEEN SUPPORTIVE?

Tell me who your friends are and I'll tell you who you are.

Surround yourself with people who have good values and goals. *Surround yourself with people who believe in you, who believe that you can.* We probably have all seen the impact of people around us. Whether we like it or not, we leave imprints on people we come across with each and every encounter.

In the biological sense, people pass diseases from one to another. In like manner, emotions are contagious, and so are attitudes. We all have been there. You spend time with someone who is grouchy and come away feeling like them. But then you connect with someone full of love, optimism, and happiness—you walk away feeling wonderful. That is why you want to be intentional about your friendships. Choose your friends carefully. *Select relationships that propel you toward your destiny.*

To have a friend you must first be a friend. Be the first one to greet and invite. *Friendliness begets friendship and in the process banishes loneliness.* To cultivate a friendly demeanor say repeatedly, "I really like him and he really likes me; we are going to have a lot of fun together." If you want someone to like you, you have to like that person first and genuinely show it.

Someone said the process of developing friendship is like playing tennis. You initiate the game by hitting the ball to the other court. If the ball comes back then you know the other player is interested in playing.

Depressed people become socially isolated and suffer loneliness. Happy people are attractive and captivating because they have what others desire. *The measure of happiness and quality people in your life depend heavily on your people skills.* Dale Carnegie's book "How to Win Friends and Influence People"[1] is a good resource in developing relationships and has helped many over the years. Happiness and people skills help surround you with quality, happy, popular, and successful people.

Having a healthy relationship is like growing a fruit tree: bugs must be removed, pruned, and constantly nurtured. It is better to have no friends than to have bad ones. A man should always keep his friendships in repair. Here are some keys to relationships: its hindrances, ways to find them, and to keep them.

Hindrances to Relationships
- Dishonesty and unreliability: failure to follow through on promises.
- Manipulation: control others' will by means other than mutual respect and consent.
- Actions that consume people's emotions and resources.
- Jealousy, criticism, condemnation, and gossip.

Ways to Find and Make Good Friends
- Be the type of person people want to get to know.
- Be a friend first.
- Initiate relationships to give, not to get.
- Talk in terms of the other person's interests and promote them first.
- Choose someone with common values.
- Look for people who, when you are with them, your best and not the worst comes out in you.
- Find someone with whom you can relax and laugh.
- Know that a friend is someone who helps you find your smile, your faith, and your confidence when you lose them in the dark.
- Look for people you can teach and learn from.

Ways to Keep Good Friends
- Be willing to give more than receive.
- Be an encourager not a criticizer.
- Be interdependent—give and take.
- Be sympathetic with friend's feelings. Generously say, "I don't blame you for feeling as you do. I would certainly feel the same way in your shoes."

- Ask questions instead of giving direct orders. Develop your questioning skill.
- Find out friend's top three desires from you and meet them.

How to Handle Disagreements or Faults

- Call attention to another's mistakes indirectly.
- Make faults seem easy to correct.
- If you are wrong, admit it quickly and emphatically.
- Talk about your own mistakes before criticizing the other.
- Deal with disagreements by *asking questions* your opponent would clearly agree on, rather than saying he is wrong.
- Always communicate and relate in ways to validate the person's core needs (love, confidence, and worth); assure him that he is fundamentally okay.
- Always approach people's mistakes in the following order:

  1. Praise
  2. Correct
  3. Encourage

When I was an adolescent, I asked my wise and influential grandma how I could make a large number of friends. I asked whether I should build friendships with those who have personalities different than mine. She said, "People are all different in personality. If you want friends who are just like you, then you'll be friendless. Build friendships with many different types of people as long as they don't try to use you. Out of those will come different circles of friends. In addition, as a general rule, give a little more than what others give you. If you give too much, you are a fool. If you are stingy, there will be no friendship."

ALEX DECIDED TO PUT GRANDMA'S ADVICE INTO GEAR.

Stay in touch with old friends and make some new ones wherever you go—especially those who are close by, i.e. next door neighbors. As the children's song goes, "Make new friends but keep the old, one is silver and the other gold."

PART 6

BE CONTENT
BUT NOT SATISFIED

CHAPTER 17

Get Your Eyes off Others

As I mentioned in the earlier chapter, I had a wonderful childhood. Nevertheless, looking back there were pockets of unhappiness I brought upon myself. Like all children, I liked toys. Next to my school were stores where toys were displayed in windows to lure children. One particular robot was popular when I was in grade school. I desperately wanted it, so I begged my parents to get it for me. It was great; the robot was even called Great Robot-X. It looked powerful. I played with it for days. But shortly after, I saw my cousins with the same robot, except theirs was BIGGER. All of a sudden mine didn't look so powerful anymore—it looked puny. When I asked my parents for the larger kind, they refused. They didn't understand what a child needed. *Don't they want me to be happy? Don't they love me?* I wondered. Not being able to suppress my desire, I lost sleep. After tossing and turning one night, the light went on in my head—*my grandmother!* I put a sad look on my face and told her how my parents were being unfair not giving me what *all* the other kids had. This worked like a charm.

Being the youngest in my family, I stayed at home while my siblings went to school. I wanted to grow up and go to work like my dad, but I also wanted to go to school and be cool like my siblings and other big kids. At first school was fun, but gradually I found myself looking forward to hearing the bell that rang at the end of each school day.

In junior high I was writing letters to my distant cousin. Both of us were at the beginning stage of puberty, and becoming interested in girls. He used to brag about his new girlfriend. Not having one, I wanted to brag too, so I told him I had five girlfriends. I hoped he wouldn't ask whether I was referring to an actual girlfriend in a romantic sense (however romantic seventh graders got back then) or those who were just friends. I was relieved when he didn't drill me on that one. He probably saw right through my poor cover up and laughed it off.

Then in high school it finally happened, my first love and cute girlfriend! It felt so cool. I followed her to her locker and then walked her to her classes like all the other cool kids. I knew other kids looked up to me. But then like the way it happened with toys in my childhood, the sense of thrill didn't last long.

Do you see a pattern? When I was in college I wanted to get out and get a real job so that I could make money and be happy. After I got a job, I was once again depressed because I wanted to get married.

I don't know how many of these cycles I went through—chasing my dream of happiness only to see it elude my grasp. It felt like as soon as I had something tasty in my mouth, I was left with sand and the taste of mud. You can probably identify with what I am describing here.

Do you recollect the time when you were desperately pursuing a particular job or project? Remember how excited you were when you got it? And what about that raise you received? How long did those thrills last? Three months? Six months? As time passed, you probably ended up feeling (unintentionally) that those good things were naturally your right. The height of your initial sense of blessing likely was lost as well. If you have a problem with the *Entitlement mentality*, then you are part of the rest of humanity.

Take our body for example. We expect our organs to naturally do their job for seventy or eighty years. Most of us are not mindful of how good our bodies have been to us amidst the busyness of our daily lives. We do not fully appreciate them—that is, until they fail to function properly.

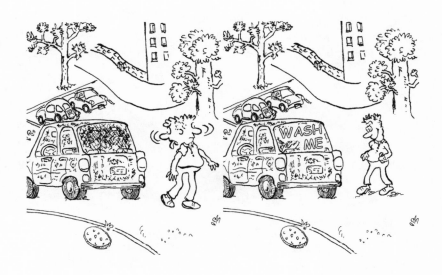

I know someone who is a gifted athlete. Both he and his younger brother were on a high school football team and their father was the coach. During one of the games, his brother was tackled by a guy who was much bigger. As a result, he became paralyzed from the neck down. The devastation was unbearable for the family. From that point my friend started being grateful, really grateful, for his arms and legs because his functioned. When was the last time you were thankful for those parts of your body?

Let's apply this same principle to the area of relationships. We expect our parents or other loved ones to be good to us and be there always, and thus do not appreciate them as much as we should—that is, until they are taken away from us—by that time it is too late to act.

The Mindset of an Unhappy Person

60-90% I want it   10-40% I have it

The Mindset of a Happy Person

60-90% I have it   10-40% I want it

Take time to be happy. If you want to be happy, you must spend time remembering the blessings you already have. How much time do you spend eating? Or spend time at the gym to be fit? To be happy you must develop gratitude muscles in your brain. And this is something you must do intentionally, on a daily basis, and as often as you can.

The development of grateful muscles in your brain occurs much the same way as the development of a healthy body. The state of health doesn't happen overnight or from a single act. It is the result of a lifetime of good diet and exercise. Similarly, sickness doesn't happen overnight either. It often occurs through repeated abuse of one's body through poor diet, lack of exercise, and a reactive lifestyle rather than one that is proactive. When you ponder over how you are already blessed, and talk about these gifts, your heart may not immediately become full with gratitude the way your stomach would after a meal. However, when this act is repeated over a period of time, you will for certain have a thankful and happy heart. You reap what you sow; every thought and word sown will sooner or later be reaped and show in your heart and actions.

MAMA!
ZEKE OVER DID
HIS GRATITUDE
WORKOUT!

A miserable person is one whose wants outweigh one's
contentment.
A happy person is one whose contentment outweigh one's
wants.

Blessed are the rich in spirit for they are filled. Those with sound mind
and humility live with a sense of fullness seeing the abundance
they've already been granted. They live content but not satisfied.
We want to train ourselves to know when to feel plentiful, and
when to adequately see needs and fill them. This however does not
occur overnight, and not without challenge.

The temptation toward discontentment plagues everyone.
People naturally think others are happier and better off than they
and envy. Singles are disgusted for lacking intimacy and
desperately pursue marriage. Those who are married praise those
who are single. Office workers compliment salesmen for being
able to travel. Meanwhile, salesmen praise office workers for being
stationed and with family more often.

This *"The grass is always greener on the other side"* syndrome occurs
from viewing others from a distance and at a slanted angle; seeing
only a part and not the whole. If you have a closer look at *the grass
on the other side*, you'll see missing patches, weeds, and at times
animal feces. It is the same way with clothes, people see how snug
clothes fit on others, but not where they pinch.

Someone said if God allows a man to rid of his disdain and
fulfill his every desire, he would be disgusted as much, or even
more, and go back to his original station. If everyone's problems
were piled, then dispersed to others, each would want his own
problem returned. Therefore, it would benefit you to focus on
your own good and misfortune of others. When we focus on what
we lack, we forget the blessings we already have.

EVERYBODY WOULD WANT HIS OWN RETURNED.

Let's look at a scenario. Let's say you acquire a new dog and you put it in your backyard. Now this dog likes to dig. It likes to hide bones you give him or kids' toys it finds in the backyard. One day you see your dog digging something in the yard, but from a distance you can't make out what it is; you just know it is foreign to you. So you go and have a closer look. The more the dog digs, the more the form takes shape. It looks like some kind of a wooden chest. Now your curiosity is raised, so you bring your shovel and start digging. It is a good size chest. Your heart starts to beat faster as you think of the possibilities of what might be in it. Finally you open it up and you find yourself choking with pure excitement. Gold, diamonds, and rubies! Yes, a treasure full of precious metals and jewels! You don't know how it found its way into your yard, but now you are the richest person in town. Imagine that, finally your luck has turned. You are totally beside yourself, but now you don't want anyone to know that such wealth is there, so you bury it again.

Now, would you forget that chest full of treasures? I doubt it. But let's suppose that in the busyness of daily affairs you do forget about it. Are the treasures still there? Are you still the richest person in town? Yes, you are, in the sense that it is in your possession. But pragmatically you are no richer than before. That is how some people live—poor in happiness even when they are really rich. Most of life's true treasures are free or can't be bought: love, health, relationships, religious liberty, and freedom of speech. Learn to prize them. *Count your blessings—ponder upon them—* treasure them.

CHAPTER 18

Be Yourself

We are all born original but die as copies.

~ Abraham Lincoln ~

Know yourself.

~ Plato ~

In 1828 in Russia there was an ugly boy. He despised his big nose, thick lips, small eyes, and long arms and said, "I am so ugly I probably will not be able to live happily." As the boy grew he realized that true beauty is found not in one's outward appearance, clothing, or what one puts on, but rather in love in its purist form. When he reached adulthood he expressed his profound discoveries in writing which became world classics. His name was Tolstoy.

It is said that fashion comes back every two to three decades. In the 70s wide leg jeans were in fashion; now they have come back again and people are starting to follow the trend. People want to do what the masses are doing. Also in the 70s it was stylish to have long hair. But in the 80s when Tom Cruise in the block buster movie *Top Gun* had a crew cut, a lot of guys styled theirs the same way. When the All-Star baseball player Randy Johnson had his head shaved, the masses followed him too.

Fashions and trends are fun to follow; however, they can also quickly and easily blur your self-identity and leave you dissatisfied with yourself. In order to live happily, you must know who you are and learn to properly love yourself.

Being yourself does not mean accepting your childish behavior. Those things must be clearly dealt with.

Being yourself means to accept the unique You as God has made you—your personality, physique, and gifts.

It is accepting what you can't change in a state of gratitude, and making changes to those things that can be made.

There are three things extremely hard:
steel, a diamond, and to know oneself.

~ Benjamin Franklin ~

The difficulty many of us face is in knowing the difference between what we can change and what we cannot. Many have benefited from what is known as The Serenity Prayer:

"God, Grant me the serenity to accept the things I cannot change, the courage to change the things I can, and the wisdom to know the difference."

What I can't change: Innate personality, body's genetic structure, IQ (Intelligence Quotient), other people.

What I can change: Mind, belief, EQ (Emotional Quotient), habits, character.

If you are a poor student of yourself, you will continually experience frustration and insecurity. Because you will try to be something you can never be, so you will experience constant frustration, condemnation, and envy. And if you try to be intimate with someone before finding your own identity, that relationship can easily become just a selfish attempt to complete yourself—to know who you are.

A flower is never meant to try to be a tree, nor should a bird try to be a cat; each are made with uniqueness—together they make our world glorious. The sooner you know and accept yourself (what you can change and can't, as well as what you are good at) the sooner you will grow in confidence, happiness, and success.

NEVER WAS DR. JEKYLL SO CONFUSED IN HIS LIFE.

Be in a Job that Is You

A great portion of our lives is either spent or affected by our jobs. If you work 40 hours per week from age 18 to 65, you will have spent about 14 percent of your life on your job. Many people work a lot more than 40 hours per week. If we calculate 60 hours of work hours per week from age 21 to 65, you will have spent approximately 22.1 percent of your life working. But that only calculates the time physically spent on the job site. If we add commute times, thoughts engaged toward your job while away from work, or extra reading done toward it—the total would probably be more like 27.3 percent.

We spend more time at work than with our loved ones, more than we sleep, more than our days of leisure. Happiness is tied a great deal with our job satisfaction. So you may ask, "What is the right job for me?" Before you can answer that question, you have to know who you are.

Knowledge of self comes easier for some than others. Very few people have outstanding abilities, or clearly know their lifetime vocational niche in their youth. For the majority of us average folks, it is one big puzzle.

To excel in a job you must have both ability and desire. Some have desire but not the ability, while others have ability but not the desire. It is those who are strong in both areas who become successful and derive the most satisfaction from their jobs.

There is a saying, "Do what you love and money will follow." To an extent that is true, because passion fully engages your faculties toward your goal. But in the real world, what you love to do may not pay adequately due to supply and demand. Or if the pay is good, it may be in a distant location away from family and friends; or the work environment may be unhealthy or hazardous. All factors must be considered since they affect the quality of your life, not just what you would enjoy doing.

CHAPTER 19

Appreciate the Little Things

Happiness consists more in small conveniences
or pleasures that occur every day, than in great
pieces of good fortune that happen but seldom.

~ Benjamin Franklin ~

One Associated Press story had on its headline, "Americans Said Healthy but Feel Lousy." The reporter, who had just had it with the current society with all of its problems, claimed that as far as he saw there wasn't one person who was truly happy. He then asked that, if there was anyone who was really happy, he should be notified of whom and what made them happy. Thousands of phone calls and letters came in, and from them they collected approximately fifty thousand happiness enhancing ideas.[1]

Surprisingly they didn't involve extraordinary events—like winning a lottery, having big promotions, or even having a lot of money or parties. Instead, they were about appreciating ordinary daily things which many of us would label as being insignificant: being grateful for who they were, what they already have, cherishing close relationships, watching the sunset, and taking walks with loved ones.

The world has always been filled with fascinating people of opposite extremes; those who felt they lacked, yet they had much, and those who had a sense of abundance, yet they owned little. No two people in history contrasted more in that regard than

Diogenes of Sinope (412-323 BC) and Alexander the Great of Greece (356-323 BC). Diogenes lived in a simple barrel much of his life to show others how people can be happy with the most basic things if accompanied with contentment. Alexander, on the other hand, conquered much of Europe and part of Asia. Yet it wasn't enough. He needed to conquer the whole world to be happy. He was reported to have said, "Had I not been Alexander, I should have liked to be Diogenes." Alexander died ahead of his time at age 33.

It was once said, "No doubt he is happy whose circumstances suit his temper, but he will be happier who can suit his temper to any circumstances. A barrel was large enough for the philosopher Diogenes, but a world was too small for a conquering Alexander."

Show me a person who is full of gratitude and I will show you a happy individual. There isn't a person whose heart is thankful yet is emotionally depressed. The cup of such a one is not only half full—it overflows. When you are thankful, you will be much happier and have more strength to face each day.

One thing that helps me is to have a list of things I am grateful for under different subject headings such as: health, relationships, finance, vocation, and politics. The more specific and detailed the list the better. I periodically go over my list and experience a continual sense of gratitude.

Lucile Blake went over her list of blessings each morning, and considered that habit one of her most precious possessions. She wasn't born with such a discipline, it happened after her near death experience. Her heart attack stopped her active lifestyle of partying, teaching, dancing, and horseback riding. She became bed ridden for a year and fought for her life. However, it was in that place of despair and pain she developed a new sense of values and inner growth.

How did she do it? She resolved to dwell only on constructive thoughts: thoughts of happiness and health. Every morning, immediately after she awoke, she forced herself to ponder on all the things she was grateful for: her daughter, her eyesight, her hearing, music on the radio, etc. Counting her blessings brought her so much joy she continued that exercise throughout her life.[2]

"I had the blues because I had no shoes,
Until upon the street, I met a man who had no feet."

PART 7

LIVE IN REALITY

CHAPTER 20

Reach High with One Foot on Earth

*The results of deferred expectations and
unfulfilled hopes are frustrations and sadness.*

Kevin was five-foot-two, a short stocky fellow in his mid-teens. He had various interests and heroes but one thing he wanted the most was to be a professional basketball player and dunk like Michael Jordan. He tried out for the basketball team at his high school but didn't make it, not even to the junior varsity. Someone told him if he tried hard enough he'd reach whatever he could dream. So day after day he went out and practiced, rain or shine. Other kids laughed at him when he told them that he would dunk and that he would become a professional basketball player. But the harder he tried, the more discouraged he became. One day, the wrestling coach saw Kevin and the courage and tenacity in him. He also observed his swiftness. He suggested Kevin try out for his wrestling team, so he did. Quick movement of his feet, keen observation of the opponent, timing of engaging—all the moves he had gained practicing basketball gave him an edge over other wrestlers. In one year he made it to the varsity team. The following year, he took second in the district championship. Then the year after that, he won the state championship.

EVER SINCE KEVIN EMBRACED REALITY AND ACCEPTED HIMSELF,
HE BEGAN TO BULLY AND INTIMIDATE BASKETBALL PLAYERS IN TOWN.

Kevin had what it took to succeed, but it was only when his expectations met what existed in the real world that he found fulfillment. We all have been there, wishing to date the most popular girl or guy in the school. Or wishing to get to know the prettiest girl or the most handsome guy, yet knowing you are outclassed.

It is good to be ambitious and set high goals but most people set themselves up for disappointment by expecting more than they can get. But you succeed only when your feet touch the ground—step by step.

One definition of insanity is to believe you can keep on believing and doing what you've been doing and get different results.

TIP

Do not try to fit the world's reality into your head. Instead, constantly analyze the real world and change your mind to fit the world's reality: facts and historical results.

What is the difference between sane and insane people? *Insane people distort the world's reality to fit into their heads.* They rely on the "experts" or simply what they have heard or been taught—opinions. *Sane people are after historical results, which shows the world's reality.* This is where the athlete's feet touch the track, the tire meets the road, and the champion boxer's swing batters the opponent.

Everyday I make a list of things to do. Like most us, I want to accomplish a lot so I end up with a long list. At the end of the day, I check off the things I accomplished. I used to get depressed during the evaluation stage because I didn't get to accomplish all that I had planned. There are basically two ways I can approach my problem, and they both work:

Solution 1:   Under plan, then add more to do once I
achieve my goals.

Solution 2:   Over plan, then take my list as a general guide,
not as an absolute requirement.

Here is how I found a solution to set goals, achieve with
maximum productivity, and feel good at the end of the day:

Under plan. I make a list of items I will absolutely meet, then
create a Nice-to-have list. This is beneficial because power and
creativity are released when one is under a certain commitment
to do something within a timeline; therefore, the majority of
my day becomes optimally productive. The little buffer time
can then be utilized as a reserve toward goals that may have
been set too high, or to take care of other things in a more
leisurely manner.

Areas of Unreasonable Expectations

Like in Kevin's case, we can have unreasonable expectations in
areas of our lives. We can have too high or too low expectations
of ourselves or other people. Typically we have too high
expectations of others and end up disappointed. I have learned it
is best to keep expectations of people low, then if they meet my
expectation it is a plus. As a result, I don't set myself up to be
depressed over someone's failure to perform.

Perhaps the most unreasonable expectations occur in marriage.
Overemphasis on romantic love from novels, movies, media, and
even the educational system lead many to falsely believe romantic
love is the basis of a good marriage. We then expect our spouse to
meet all our unmet past needs, which they can't possibly do.

We create an ideal picture of what our spouse should be, then we work hard to mold them into this ideal figure. When a gap exists between the "real" and "ideal", frustration and disappointment occur and the marriage suffers.

It's not only in the area of marriage. Many of us put unrealistic pressure on ourselves to perform. When we don't meet our "ideal," we feel like failures. Pursuing excellence is good, but falling into a "perfectionistic" mentality results in devastation. A good way to escape this way of thinking is to take a hard look at your current performance level. Then make that your baseline for setting goals. What I mean is this, *take an average of your performance in a given area, and then set your performance bar a little above that*, but not much higher. Once you achieve it, then you can raise the bar a little higher again. This will help you feel continually like a winner.

CHAPTER 21

Live in the Present Moment

Sally was an attractive young woman. She had been married to a young man of her dreams for several years. But for some unknown reason she was unable to have an intimate relationship with her husband. She loved him but couldn't stand it when he initiated sex. She made an effort to change this about herself but couldn't.

One day she had a dream. In it she saw herself running all alone on a wooded trail. She recognized it as her favorite place to get fresh air away from the city. The fall breeze felt cool on her face and the birds chirped all around her as she made her way down the tree-lined path. It was peaceful and quiet.

All of a sudden a dark shadow came from behind and took her down. She cried for help but the location was too isolated for anyone to hear. After she woke up, she was filled with rage and screamed, "I hate you! I will never let another man touch me as long as I live!"

As she processed her dream, she realized she had deeply buried her painful past under the guilt and regret of having put herself into this dangerous situation. As long as she was chained to the past and held her bitterness, she could not engage in a healthy relationship with her husband. Although it was difficult, she made a choice to change. She decided not to let the painful past keep her ruining her present. The recovery was a trying process, and with the help of her counselor, she was able to open herself up and engage in intimacy with her husband who loved her very much.

In another case, Joel had good things going for him. His new career in sales was going well. He was married to a lovely wife, and although his kids got themselves into trouble at times as kids do, they were fairly well behaved. Then one day Joel's father, whom he admired and wanted to please, said Joel needed to work harder and make more money, if he wanted to be happy.

By nature being a high achiever and extremely goal oriented, Joel took on the challenge of being financially free. Being financially free meant he could retire early, buy his children sports cars so they could be the cool kids at their school. He also thought about how nice it would be to have something tangible to brag about at his next high school class reunion. So he began doing overtime at work, he ran a side business on weekends, and he even took some night classes.

The money started rolling in, then lots of it. But not long after, tension started to build between his wife Cassy, and him. She complained he wasn't spending enough time with her and his family. But Joel was set on his goal, because he believed if they could be financially free, they would be happy.

The more Cassy confronted him the harder he worked because he thought the quicker he reached his goal the quicker she would see what he and his father knew. The tension then escalated when Joel's son was caught doing drugs at school. His wife felt it was due to the absence of fatherhood. When the situation did not improve, the whole thing was too much for Cassy, so she filed for a divorce. Then Joel, at age forty, found himself at a counselor's office. While discussing his situation with the therapist, he had tears streaming down his face, "My father told me that if I made my first million I would be happy. He lied to me!"

At times the nature of our work makes it difficult to immediately adjust life's priorities. Commitments and deadlines don't allow for time with family. Local and international competition is intense. Younger people are constantly emerging in our fields with a technological edge and are willing to do more while charging less. If you lose your spot in the race, what would you do in this difficult economy? How would you provide for your family? You come home under heavy stress and exhaustion with these thoughts going through your mind only to have your spouse yell at you. She blames you for her own frustrations which she didn't get to vent toward someone else that day.

Amidst these challenges you want to plan for tomorrow but live for today. Yesterday is past and tomorrow doesn't exist yet. If you put the "Only if" condition on being joyful, you'll never attain it. Today alone is real and by being proactive, I can build the future I want.

Overemphasis on the past—whether failures or successes can keep you chained there. *The only time you should look back is when you need to learn from it* so you can more effectively live in the present.

Overemphasis on the future will result in worry and imagined fears; repetitive language of such a person is, "someday … when this or that occurs, then I will be happy." But that someday will never come if you do not focus on living in the present.

Overemphasis on the present, however, while neglecting the past and the future can leave you naive, lazy, poor, and a glutton.

Live in the Present Moment

If you don't give proper emphasis to each of these three areas, you live in an unreal and unproductive and frustrating world. Let us live productively. Plan for the future but live in the present. Learn from the past but be in the present. The key word is *focus*. Past, present, and future are all part of us, but where is your focus?

NATURAL INSTINCTS

It is a trait of unhappy people to be in the wrong places at the wrong times—and there they remain enslaved. Someone asked an old man why he was planting a tree when he may not live to see it grow much. He replied saying he isn't planning on dying tomorrow and as long as he is planning on living he would plan for tomorrow. Live in the present and you will have all the strength needed to face every day.

Focus not on the past but on the present for the future.

Nick Vujicic

An Inspiration for a Ridiculously Good Life

When you're born without limbs, you can't just take
a pill and expect to deal with the devastation.
There is no such pill.

If you are one of those who find life challenging, you are part
of the company of everyone on earth. Now imagine yourself
needing to face your daily tasks but having to do them without use
of your arms. No arms or hands to hold and carry objects, to hug
a family member or friends; no fingers to experience touch or
write. How much more difficult would everyday be? Now imagine
if instead of no arms, you had no legs. No ability to dance, walk,
run, or even stand. Now put both of those scenarios together—
no arms and no legs. How much weight would that add to your
day-to-day life?

In the year 1982 in Melbourne, Australia, without any medical
explanation or warning, Nicholas Vujicic came into the world with
neither arms nor legs. The first sight of their newborn baby was
quite a shock. A limbless son was not what nurse Dushka Vujicic
and her husband, Pastor Boris Vujicic, had been expecting. What
would the future hold for their son, they wondered?

Being abnormal was incredibly difficult. Nick struggled with
deep depression and loneliness as he dealt with the challenges of
school, bullying, and self-esteem issues. He constantly faced such
a difficult question as why he was different than all the other kids
surrounding him; why had he to be the one born without arms and
legs. He wondered what the purpose behind his life was, or if a
purpose even existed. At age ten he tried to drown himself in his
bathtub but did not go through with it out of love for his family.

Still, nothing gave him peace. According to Nick, the turning
point was when he responded yes to God's question, "Do you

194

trust me?" He realized people with arms and legs lacked peace too, so having limbs was not the solution. He decided to trust God, accept what he can't change, and change his attitude.[1]

Little did he and his parents know that years later he would be someone who would inspire and motivate millions of people from all around the world. Nick pursued academics and obtained a double bachelor's degree, majoring in accounting and financial planning at Griffith University in Logan, Australia. By the age of 19, Nick started to fulfill his dream of being able to encourage other people and bring them the news of hope through motivational speaking and sharing his testimony about how God changed his life and gave him a future and a hope. "I found the purpose of my existence, and also the purpose of my circumstance. There's a purpose for why you're in the fire." Nick wholeheartedly believes that there is a purpose in each of the struggles we encounter in our lives and that our attitude towards those struggles, along with our faith and trust in the Lord, can be the keys to overcoming the challenges we face.

Today, this limbless young man is the President and CEO of a non-profit organization, Life Without Limbs. Since his first speaking engagement back when he was 19, Nick has traveled around the world, sharing his story with millions of people. He has spoken to various groups such as students, teachers, businessmen and women, and entrepreneurs. He has also been interviewed on TV programs worldwide. "If God can use a man without arms and legs to be His hands and feet, then He will certainly use any willing heart!"

CONCLUSION

CHAPTER 22

A Choice

Most people are about as happy as
they make up their minds to be.

~ Abraham Lincoln ~

One of the respected leaders in Korean history was a Buddhist monk named Jin. As a young man, Jin wanted to reach a higher spiritual aspiration, so he traveled toward a reputable monastery in China. The mountain paths were treacherous and long. One late evening, he found an old abandoned house. Too dark to go further, he decided to lodge there for the night. Once inside, he quickly fell asleep. In the middle of the night, Jin awoke to thirst, so he looked around the room. He was delighted to find a bowl of water glistening under the moonlight. Water was refreshing beyond words.

The next morning, sun shined brightly in the room. As he arose, he couldn't believe what he saw. The bowl he drank from was a human skull! In horror and disgust he coughed and threw up vehemently.

Later when he regained his composure, he asked, *how did water that tasted divine turn bitter?* It dawned on him; life's key is in one's mind. Reality doesn't matter as much as one's perception of reality. People build pleasure and torment, heaven and hell; they do that in their minds, and experience them by their choices.

Jin didn't need to go to China or to the end of the earth to find happiness. He needed to further explore this amazing discovery, so he journeyed back home. "There is nothing either good or bad," said Shakespeare, "but thinking makes it so."

It was traumatic news, but Rolf Benirschke, a kicker for the San Diego Chargers, was diagnosed with Crohn's disease—an incurable illness. "It sounds like a cliché, I know. But when you've been very ill, the good things look different. I love the beautiful sunshine we have here in San Diego. I love laughing and being around people. And yes, I love kicking footballs again."

Benirschke spent long days in the hospital. Nevertheless, he got himself to practice. Severe pain and weight loss seemed to be no respecter of persons. When they ran him over like a Mack truck, he mustered his courage and got right back up.

"I kept on playing because athletes are supposed to play with pain. In spite of my weakened condition, I managed to make it through the first four games of the season," he said.

He then was hospitalized again and went through two major operations. After spending one month in the hospital, he came back home weighing only 125 pounds. In the new football season, the Chargers named Benirschke an honorary captain for the Pittsburgh Steelers' game.

"That was the beginning," he remembered. "I decided I was going to come back ... I began with little steps, unimaginably slow, by walking on the beach."

He then took on bigger steps. He ran, swam, and lifted weights—there was no stopping him. When the next season approached he was 180 pounds solid.

"I remember the first game I played last season," he said. "I thought back to all those moments when I was watching the games from the hospital bed. When I got back out there on the field again, I thought to myself, 'Amazing. Here I am again.' "

That year, Benirschke was ranked second in the NFL, scoring 118 points. He made 24 of 36 field goal attempts. The following year was even more spectacular. He hit 19 of 26 field goals and helped his San Diego Chargers reach the American Conference Championship game.

TRAP

 If you look to circumstantial changes for happiness you will never be happy.

Benirschke chose to determine the future he wanted and he attained it. Yes, the outcome of his action was exceptional but so was his attitude. Everyday you will face problems. *When winds of adversity blow against your sail, it is the choice you make and how you react that will determine whether the wind will be adverse or favorable.* It is your decision to consciously choose the right attitudes and behaviors, and to live by the principles shared in this book. They will result in happiness over unhappiness.

Our universe is governed by laws; by observing them, we experience joy—or in ignoring them, we suffer. What helps me to understand this is the imagery of a room full of furniture. The furniture exists whether the light is on or off. If you attempt to move through the room with the light off you will likely stumble over the furniture and you may get injured. However, if the light is on, you will be able to see and safely weave your way around every obstacle. The purpose of what was shared in this book has been to shed light for you to see these principles that are invisible to the physical eye but, are nevertheless real. And in seeing them you will work with them to your advantage.

TIP

 Choose to be happy being who you are and with what you have, right here and now.

As I conclude, I would like to humbly confess, that although I've come a long way, I still struggle in living out the principles I shared with you in this book. I have learned that it is not something that happens overnight, it takes time, not because the information can't be absorbed quickly, but because it takes time to live them out. I know that the state of complete happiness is not attainable in this life—placing my hope of attaining it in the life following gives me a great comfort. In the end, we all choose what lives inside us. Yesterday is gone, tomorrow does not yet exist—only today is reality. Make everyday count. Decide today that you will not settle for a life of mediocrity. Envision the glorious life you have been dreaming of by putting the principles we discussed in this book into gear. Make a commitment to yourself; that from this day forward, you are going to be rich in happiness!

Notes

Chapter 1: You Can Learn to be Happy

1. Wilt Chamberlin, *A view from Above* (New York: Signet Penguin Group, 1992), p. 258.

2. Daniel Goleman, *Emotional Intelligence* (New York: Bantam Books, 1997), pp. 6-7.

   Daniel Goleman, *The Brain Manages Happiness And Sadness in Different Centers* (New York Times, March 28,1995), Science. http://www.nytimes.com/1995/03/28/science/the-brain-manages-happiness-and-sadness-in-different-centers.html Accessed on January 04, 2013.

Chapter 3: Causes of Unhapiness

1. Archibald Hart, *15 Principles For Achieving Happiness* (Dallas: Word, 1988), p. 120.

2. Lepper, M. R., Greene, D., and Nisbett, R. E. (1973). Undermining children's intrinsic interest with extrinsic reward: A test of the "overjustification" hypothesis. Journal of Personality and Social Psychology, 28: 129-37.

3. James Dobson, *Dare to Discipline* (Carol Stream: Tyndale House Publishers, 1992), p. 59.

Chapter 5: See Your Future Here

1. Charles J. Givens, *Super Self* (New York: Simon & Schuster, 1993). *Success talk* Book on Cassette (Nightingale Conant 1992).

Chapter 6: How to Grow a Rich Attitude

1. Steve Jobs, Commencement Address at Stanford University. http://news.stanford.edu/news/2005/june15/jobs-061505.html Published on June 14, 2005. Accessed on March 10, 2014.

Chapter 10: Hey You Good Looking!

1. Dr. Martyn Lloyd Jones, *Healing and the Scriptures* (Nashville: Oliver Nelson, 1988), p. 50.

2. George Vaillant, Harvard University.
    http://news.harvard.edu/gazette/2001/06.07/01-happywell.html
    Published on June 07, 2001. Accessed on March 10, 2014.

3. Howard E. Ferguson, *The Edge* (Cleveland: Getting the Edge Company,1991), p. 6-14.

4. Dr. Martyn Lloyd Jones, *Healing and the Scriptures* (Nashville: Oliver Nelson, 1988), p. 148.

5. Daniel Goleman, *Emotional Intelligence* (New York: Bantam Books, 1997), pp. 170-173.

Chapter 14: Value Principle

1. Daniel Goleman, *Emotional Intelligence* (New York: Bantam Books, 1997), pp. 80-83.

Chapter 15: Life is a Team Sport

1. Time, *20th Century Blues* (New York: Aug. 28, 1995).

2. Daniel Goleman, *Emotional Intelligence* (New York: Bantam Books, 1997), p. 178.

Chapter 16: Surround Yourself with Happy People

1. Dale Carnagie, *How to Win Friends and Influence People* (New York: Simon & Schuster, Reissue edition 2009).

Chapter 19: Appreciate the Little Things

1. Star News, 18 February 1988.

2. Dale Carnagie, *Stop Worrying and Start Living* (New York: Simon & Schuster, Reissue edition, 1984), p. 141.

Chapter 21: Live in the Present Moment

1. Nick Vujicic, *Life Without Limits* (WaterBrook Press, 2012). pp 45, 54.

Recommended Reading

How to Win Friends and Influence People, *by Dale Carnagie*

Stop Worrying and Start Living, *by Dale Carnagie*

The Edge, *by Howard E. Ferguson*

Reach us online at WWW.RICHINYOU.COM

Made in the USA
Charleston, SC
01 November 2014